ARCADIO

A
Novel
by
William Goyen

Clarkson N. Potter, Inc. / Publishers
DISTRIBUTED BY CROWN PUBLISHERS, INC., NEW YORK

PUBLISHED BY CLARKSON N. POTTER, INC.,
One Park Avenue, New York, New York 10016 and simultaneously in
Canada by General Publishing Company Limited

Manufactured in the United States of America

Library of Congress Cataloging in Publication Data
Goyen, William.
Arcadio.
I. Title.
PS3513.097A77   1983   813'.54   83-3939
ISBN 0-517-55053-9

Design by Gael Towey Dillon

10 9 8 7 6 5 4 3 2

FIRST EDITION

To the Vine
and
The Palm
and
for Doris

The author wishes to express his gratitude to John Igo,
Reginald Gibbons, and Deirdre Simone-Hill for their
loving help with this work.

Portions of this novel, in different form, have appeared in
The Southwest Review and *TriQuarterly*.

The Knocking Figure
at the Door

JUST TODAY I CAME upon the picture postcard. It fell out of a book that I had not opened for years.

I had found the painting in a London museum, stood before it and remembered Uncle Ben, long gone. In the museum shop I had bought the postcard reproduction of the painting and took it for my own, as Uncle Ben took it long ago for his and lost it. I must have found it again for him.

Today I have so long gazed upon the picture, here in a faraway place, in an ancient holy city far from my own place where I first heard Uncle Ben's unexpected story and where Uncle Ben lies now in the ground with his ancestors, and mine, many who, with me, had heard his sudden story that long-ago summer night; I have today so long gazed upon that picture that I have come into a vision—an "apparition" my mother would have called it—made of true memory and outrageous fabrication. And that is what I have to tell, what has risen up so long later from the image hidden early in my mind by Uncle Ben's story and freed by the picture postcard of the beautiful painting called *The Light of the World.*

Early Visitors
to My Solitude

NE TIME ON A HOT July night when we were sitting in the dark hoping to get a breath of breeze, I heard my mother whisper, "There's somebody standing out in the yard." In the flare of the heat lightning we saw a figure streaming down its whole body with hair struck full of quivering light, with hair of light streaming down to the ground and eyes as glowing as lanterns.

"'Tis a visitation," said the woman Carrie, our friend who lived with us. "The Bible tells us that word."

"An apparition," said my mother; and my father called it something out of the woods, drawn out of the deep woods by the light of our house. My sister said it was a big moth and it did look something like that.

But whatever the thing was, it glowed out its pale lamps of eyes at us and streamed down its lighted hair. I was not afraid but pitied it. My father cried "Ho!" and then the little dog who had been paralyzed with fear was given voice to bark, and the light of the shy visiting stranger was gone.

All night I thought the figure might be out there,

darkened, its light put out by our fear. I lay awake and thought about it, about turned-away things, things not taken, things thrown back or let go, or the light in them put out by fear. At the window, on my knees, I sought the light of the beautiful visitor, wherever it was, far away in the dark woods or nearby on the sandy road that went past our house, on the black railroad tracks leading off into gloom beyond the distant house on the rise of land; or very close, right in the yellow jasmine bush that my mother's mother planted when she was a bride in this house, the sweet flowering bush of summer nighttime, just there by the window—could the turned-away caller, man-woman, saint-devil, comforter and disturber, be there, just at the window? My feelings were human and divine. I wanted the streaming figure to lie close to my body in my bed, touch my body which burned for touching and was so secret to me—how much longer could I bear the secret, keep my body a secret to others, consecrated only to myself? It is said we leave home—go out—at the urge of our young soul; but it is just as much to break the secret of our body, in its name we go. Yet I longed for the blessed stranger to restore my soul, which seemed lost.

We had seen other mysterious strangers in the remoteness of our place. They had come to us out of the black summer nights that stung us with heat and kept us sitting up most of the night, half-drugged between sleep and waking, together in the darkness where we were each one alone, solitary sleeper each; or in the windy, starlight, spring nights—a knocking, a shadowed face, a hand held out at the back door: a gypsy girl, dark and spiteful, a gentle beggar from the road, a hobo off the freight train that ran past our house, a drunken logger from sawmill town, and once what turned out to be an escaped woman convict run away from Huntsville Pen driven by longing to see her child in Houston. What the feeling was that they left in me, in memory, was their shyness, a giving out from them, though they were asking, and a moment of beauty. Shy beauty surrounds those times in my memory, not fear. And it seemed that for that moment, in which we gave the stranger something, there was an exchange of love, that we were visited by love, not fear. Others spoke of calling the "deputy" (whatever that was) and of putting a shotgun by the door at night.

And there once had come a daring old bearded person in the afternoon, who stood by the woodpile and looked and looked at us and did not come closer. He had come soundlessly, in an October afternoon, when apples were purple on our trees and blue smoke hung in the distances, what for, he would not answer when the question was called out to him. His look was that look I cannot describe, although I see it over and over in my memory and I have seen it a few times more, as my life has gone on, on the faces of the unexpected at that still and awesome moment of recognition. And I try, again, to tell what it was like—that look; that look on the face of those sudden visitors appearing before me: it was shy, it was tender, it gave radiant love, it gave union not alienation, asking, not questioning, it gave fearlessness not fear, those visitors' (they would not stay) faces, eyes, mouth, dear hair, that came before me in my life, to bring me fresh sense of life, and to go on.

Another was a sprightly figure who looked at us as though we were intruding upon him, sitting in our pomegranate tree at summer noon. When we came he looked down at us with mischief in his eye. He seemed to be at home in the pomegranate tree. He wore a curious hat with a bird's feather in it and some kind of a jacket made of faded purple satin on which something sparkling caught the bright noon sunlight. He was a sight in the pomegranate tree. While we watched him, after a long cordial, almost bemused, stare, the person descended gracefully from the tree and looking at us again straight on, with that look, went on his way. We watched him disappear on the road.

"It's the orphan boy, grown up," someone said. "That used to live with Leota Barnes, up towards the cotton gin, but then ran away to live in the bottomlands."

"Seems happy enough," another said. "Sitting up in our pomegranate tree like he planted it."

"Peculiar persons living in this part of the world," my father said. "East Texas's a peculiar part of the world. Peopled with some peculiarities you wouldn't guess were here, coming as a surprise to people that live outside—and even to us that live inside, sometimes. Must be the river and the riverbottoms, parts of it wild and forbidden, and the Thicket. Seeing men in ten-gallon hats and cowboy boots in town talking cattle and cotton—that's only the way it looks; there's more than that."

And then Uncle Ben said, quietly as if out of a dream, "Once while hunting rabbit by the dry river I come upon a person bathing itself in a pool of Trinity River. I seen it. I crouched down in the weeds and couldn't believe my eyes. At first I said it's a baptism in the river, a person's baptizing themselves, I said. And I saw it quietly washing in the river hardly making a sound except for the soft comforting sound that only rustling water makes, yet tis, too, like the sound a bird will make in the deep nighttime when you're sleeping in the woods

and will lie there and hear it, almost as if tis to console
you, almost like a mothering sound or of something being
taken care of making it feel safe and peaceful—a peaceful
sound is what it is that water makes when it's handled
and picked up and tossed and breaks against flesh like the
beautiful body I come upon standing knee deep in the
clear spring water there at the hidden place where the
river used to flow under the trees. And there I saw it
slowly bending to pick up water and scatter it over its
beautiful body, scattering the water and the water could
have been something like sand or soft grain, the person
could have been in a field; except there is nothing else in
the world like spring water, is its own special thing unto
itself, pure spring water, isn't it? I love spring water, love
all water, and it's a wonder, too, considering how Mama
almost drownded in the river and acarrying me six
months inside her womb, I know the feeling water can
make me have. Twas just at sundown. Twas so beautiful
is all I can say. Just wish I had the words for it or had a
picture of it. What I did was not to disturb the strange
beautiful person, was to very quietly rise up from the
high grass and go away. To let the person alone, to let
the beautiful body alone. I didn't want to go. I looked
back and saw, in the early twilight that was already falling, the bending and gathering and tossing figure, glis-
tening with water, washing itself as if twas making slow
dancing movements and twas only washing itself; and
then twas when I saw that it twas part a man and part a
woman, the man part was sweetly washing the woman
part and the woman sweetly the man, the woman part
baptizing the man and the man baptizing the woman.
How twas so holy and how twas so flesh, the body of this

WILLIAM GOYEN

6

being was so holy and so flesh, I was divided in two almost by my feelings from it. How it had such respect for itself and give such tenderness to itself was what hurt me so, twas like a sudden hurt in my breast to witness such tenderness, and yet I was apanting so and had all kinds of feelings that I still so sharply remember. And I turned again to go and leave the beautiful bather. And saw then, in that time of day—twas in early May I recollect—how lonely it was and saw suddenly how lonely everything there was, in that time of day, the sundown, the last of Trinity River run down to just a pool, all the powerful springs that had made a long river running through the bottomlands gone down to just one trickling one, and the last bather in it, like the ghost of the lost river, like all humanity bathing together in it, all men, all women, for the last time, in Trinity River. This is what I felt, and the rustling sound of the water, the beautiful place and the peace and the sadness, that I never forgot. And there under a willow tree I found the bather's things. They were an old army officer's uniform neatly folded, and a cap, and a Bible written in Mescan, once white but now yellowed, and from that yellowed white Bible there fell out upon the ground what I took away, stole I guess because I had to have it, a picture card faded in its colors and soiled from a lot of handling. It showed gentle Jesus knocking at a door in the night and holding a burning lantern in the night and said *The Light of the World*. And I saw on the back written in a big handwriting a strange name: *Arcadio*. I had to have this picture and I took it with me, wish I had it now but lost it somewhere through the years, lost it, maybe when I rode on the train that time up to Crockett to see the side doctor, to have a complete physical cause of that pain kept griping me in my side, maybe on that trip was when I lost the picture, oh wish I had it now."

Everyone was quiet and no one said another word. Then Ben said finally, "Wish I had a picture of it, wish I had it on my dresser and could look at it, the holy sight in the river, naked, naked. Twas—well, just a feeling I never had before and not again since, I guess, until just now when I've told it, more than I could ever find a word for, don't know what, to this day, exactly, and that was oh I guess fifty years ago, by this time the beautiful bather must be dead and buried in its grave. But now somebody else will know its story cause I've told it, and I'm glad."

And then my Uncle Ben, a man I knew was going soon to die—I'd heard the whispering about it—and lately had been saying peculiar things, sometimes black and dreadful, out of an obsessive remembering, went slowly on away.

I knew so little about him—how could I know except what I overheard and what I imagined: he had gone away early in passion to some promise, against all pleading, and lost the promise, and came back, made dumb. We had never before—and then suddenly—heard him speak like that; sometimes a person finally finds the song out of what had struck him dumb long before; and later I heard a person say that such a time is the time of Grace, of reconciliation with the will of God after long pain of lost promise, and I believe that Uncle Ben had found the song that summer night and was, for those moments of his found song, in the grasp of such a time; and his song was a parting song, a song of farewell. So had Arcadio in my vision of him found his *adiós*—voice to sing a sweet goodbye, and after his own long dumbness.

WILLIAM GOYEN

8

Then Aunt Evelina said, "Ben was drinking. Never hunted a rabbit in his life sober."

"Twas a Sideshow escaped from a Carnival," another voice explained.

That night I could not sleep because of the extraordinary visitation to our ordinary place that Uncle Ben had surprisingly told of. I was haunted by visions of the beautiful being. I felt its presence. It beckoned me. I wanted at once to go into the night to the riverbottoms in search of the beautiful being Arcadio, long long dead, to wait under the willows in expectation of its appearance. What beings there were in the world, and had been! Magical and mysterious and hidden, not plain and easy and available like people in the town, saying "Hoddy Son how's your folks?" I was ready now, full, where I had been in preparation before, I would without question go away with it, into the magical world where all the other visitors to my solitude dwelt. For this I called softly through the window, into the blue personal moonlight of our local midnight. I left a futile call, long ago and long too late, "Arcadio! Arcadio! Come back to our place! Come back!"

In a rapture, that night, I saw that the strange being had come to the window by my bed. I saw in the gentle moonlight its face glowing through the trembling curtains that the midnight breeze touched. It was all hot and luring. I was stirred to an excitement I had never known, a surging, now, of that earlier faintly touching excited fear and wanting, touching at my breast, and down below my belly in the tenderest part of me. The face and drawing presence of the beautiful naked bather demanded something of me I had never given.

"Is your heart right?" I heard it whisper. "You got to

get your heart right, Son. Because we are living in the Last Days! It is the End Time, the Rapture is coming."

The being of the beautiful body was imploring me to consider my soul, to look after my salvation at the end of things. Yet I hadn't even begun! I was fresh, daily charged with powers that were ripening me, I was new, my body was beginning to glow, there were secret moistures, there was new soft hair, there was a promise of a coming rapture that would deliver me of what had grown to be unbearable swelling of my senses. Yet the beautiful visitor spoke of the salvation of my soul, of the Last Days, the Rapture of the End of the World. My world! Soon to end just when it was soon to begin! And my annunciator of the last days of the world was my very tempter, my very invitation to my beginning, to my first days!

I whispered back to my visitor through the moonlit window, "But how do you know? How do you know that these are the Last Days of the World?"

"Omens, promises, prophecies coming to pass— hens crowing, women whistling, man's greed and the murder of fresh water." My visitor pronounced its doom in a voice that was melodious.

And after an awful time of silence, I whispered, trembling, "Make my heart right! Save my soul! But let me see your body again."

But it was gone.

I did not tell my Uncle Ben about my vision of Arcadio. In the days that followed his story and my dream I watched him, dumb again and staying far apart, sitting sometimes in the field under the live oak tree. Within another year my Uncle Ben was dead and gone. But this was what I heard and what I saw and all I had with which to make the story that follows, if you will read it or hear the song of it, although time stopped it until just today, many years later. For within some more years I was gone, in my own passion and toward my own promise. I never came back again.

But today as I've held the picture postcard before me, that place and those people are live in my memory, that summer night hums in heat and music in my head: I see again that dark gathering of stilled listeners. They heard a mysterious song sung only once. Those listeners are gone, all but one, and the first singer is gone but not the song. I sing it again. *Canto*.

In my vision I went to the riverbottom—twas in early May, I recollect. I was headed toward the wondrous bather's pool when I begun to hear the faint music, silvery and watery and softly throbbing, and it was like a warmth around my head and face and seemed to come out of my own head, music of my own. It softly pulled me through the palmettos and the dewberries and the crawling vines. And then when I looked up I saw the early-morning specter of the old abandoned railroad trestle. Aloft against the hot blue sky, vaulted higher than I ever remembered it, held ascendant by frail legs rising out of the green willows and wateroaks of the bottomland, aloft and slender and as fragile as if it were made of paper, hung the condemned trestle, a lonesome bridge of orange-colored rails and gray ties that weather had taken over after the trains were forbidden, a lonesome pier reaching over a white riverbed of shell, vanishing into a green billow of woods, a crossing of dreams, of secret trespasses, flights of ghosts and fairies, and since it was removed from the dead weight of iron was now the fragile avenue of weightless things, slide of snakes, feet of frogs and tread of birds, the passing over of groundless, footless things, motes and beams and flowers of floating snow, and winged seeds and blown crystals of rain, a transfer for winds and fogs and aerial lights and fires.

And there I saw the being sitting under the trestle, in the latticed light, leaning against a leg of the trestle that, although it stood in the white shell of the dry riverbed, was green and garlanded with blooming vines, woven with trumpetvine and honeysuckle and morning-glory, like a Maypole. He was dressed in an old army uniform. An officer's cap was aslant on his head and he had a harmonica clasped between his lips, blowing and sucking and fluttering an odd tune.

All of a sudden the music stopped and the figure stood up and spoke to me out of the pale green latticed light from the wild bower in the dry shell. And it was very strange and was not like anything I had ever laid my eyes on; it was fearful, it was strange.

3

A Singer at Large

Y NAME IS ARCADIO, and I will not do you no harm, come under the shade of this old rayroad trestle if you wan to. Train's gone. *Por favor: siéntase,* set down please, here by the blooming vines of morningglory and honeysuckle that smells so sweet in the morning sun, here in the bed of the river, white bed of shell, river's gone too. You look like you been walkin for some time in the hot riverbottom through the palmettos and the dewberries and the crawling vines, *siéntase.* Set down. If you wan to.

How did you find me did you hear my tune did you come to where the frenchharp played, tis an old tune you heard acomin from the dead river's bed, "The Waltz of the Spotted Dog," my old tune that I played out in the Show, a sad waltz, some folks have said that tis the same tune as "Missouri Waltz" if you have ever heard a tune called that, "Missouri Waltz"; tis not, tis not the same tune, *compadre.* When I was in the Show. And never said a word, only sound my breath made was through this little harp, played it once for each Show, Old Shanks made me do it, well did keep me awake and showed I had some talent. Sometimes tears of my eyes run down into the little harp, I blew the music through my tears, a watery sound for a *vals*, this little *arpa* harp is rusted from the salt of my tears, little salted frenchharp. When tears dry up their salt bites deep as rust. Ever see that on something? Makes a little speckle of rust. Tears can rust, *compadre*. Hope you never had to cry too many. You wan hear.

Cantando, compadre. Canto. But there was a long time when I didn't sing no song. I am at large. Which is how they called me on the radio when I was found missing. At large. There is no Mescan word for it. *Cantor soy.* I think of myself as a singer. A singer at large. I had not been free in all *mi vida*, that's the Mescan word for life, until I excaped. Locked up by my father Hombre, locked up by the Chinaman Shuang Boy, locked up by Old Shanks in the Show. All of which I will tell you, singing my song. Come under the trestle and listen if you wan to, in the shade of the morningglory vine in the morning, God knows how it blooms so fresh without no water; or go on, if you wan to. I am bidding a sweet *adiós* to civilization, old world is wearing down, *Corazón*. What have they done to this place? I got a sweet goodbye to sing to it. *Pasa el mundo viejo, se pasa.* Old world is passing away. Meantime, I keep an eye out for my mother. Sounds funny but that is the words for it, keep an eye out, that is the Anglo espression. We have no such Mescan espression.

I am used to sitting silent under the public gaze as a serene listener. I was not allowed to speak back to my gazers nor answer their questions. Away from my gilded chair of serenely listening, I now sit in an open place and sing free. An at-large singer. You listen if you wan hear it.

If not, the air is my listener, leaves and birds my hearers. I listened to the world, now world hear me is what I'm thinking! *Qué dice Arcadio? Qué dice el Mundo?* God knows the years my ears heard whispers and soft calls. *Muñeco! Chingame! Corazón Dulce!* Show it to me! Fuck me! Filthy people of cheap towns. Sometimes a person alone in the tent with me would stand before me and tell me his trouble. My wife she run off with another man; my little baby turned out deaf and dumb, are you a healer can you lay on hands. As if I was a Buddha or *San José* Saint Joseph—or *Santa Teresa.* Sometimes one of my gazers would implore. *Comprendes?* You wan hear? Sometimes I would be supplicated in whispers. But I do not now supplicate nor implore. My song serenely sing, *cantando,* is the way I look at it. And I keep an eye out for *mi madre,* which is an espression, keeping out an eye, *comprendes.*

On most days I have me some *paz.* Peace. It was not so before. I wan be on the road, peaceful, I said, to be wandering in the woods and prairies, in the liveoaks and bluebonnets of my old home, I wan beg for my supper and lay in the fields, I said, be with the stars and the streams, sit all day if I wan to, in the shade, see Texas, see Texas down around the Boca Chica down around there, if I wan to, at Brownsville and down around there, I said. And ask about my mother over at San Antone, although I have a feeling that she met an early death. I am dressed in this old army officer's uniform of some old war, man said to me that give it to me outside of some town said that he don know where tis from, an old war, said don know which, man said; give me the cap too; nor do I know the name of the town. I am *contento* in this old war uniform and I am clean, I dote on cleanliness, I bathe in rivers and keep my body fresh and I wash my clothes in waters of streams when I can find them without any brown foam afloating, what is that shit? Who did all that? What in God's name have they put into the rivers and the streams?—where they happen to run water, most of them are dry—who let them do that to the waters? Put all that shit in the waters? I beg for bread at doors, to know a part of human charity though I'm pretty rich in my own right *porque* I saved my money in the Show. Which I carry privately, rob me if you wan to, I feel too gentle to resist, I am a peaceful person walking towards God. You'd never find it anyway, *oyente,* listener.

I try to stay out of the stinking cities—who did that, who put all the cars? Ought to catch em and throw em into the rivers of shit, that put all the cars. You wan hear? I am near the little town where I was born, in Texas, where I lived before my mother left me. I know that I am now outside that town because I remember this trestle rising up high out of the river waters, today when first I come upon it trestle was higher to me than ever I remembered it and its long thin legs comin up out of the old bottomland seemed like twas made of paper when first I seen it, lonesome bridge of orange rails and gray ties, tis a lonesome pier areachin over a white riverbed of shell, a *visión* seemed to me when first I seen it, seen the trestle. And under the trestle as I got closer come bloomin up out of the white shell of the dry riverbed morningglories and honeysuckles and trumpetvines all abloomin in the early morning light. And into this *visión* I took my seat, sat down to rest and play my frenchharp. And you come.

And I remember the train passin over and the blue thicket of trees where are they all now who did this seems like somebody burnt up a lots of the trees, dry trees lots of dry trees among the green ones I hate a dry tree, Devil got it. And greedy rich men helped him. And I know I am now outside that little town where I was borned because I hear the rumble of it, must have grown severely for I don remember a rumble when I lived there with *mi madre* Chupa before she run away. Who did that? I never been back since, after my mother run away from us, for my father Hombre took me on to a town that I will later sing you if you wan hear it, if not I'll tell it to the air, as I have said earlier, it is the singing that is important to me. I wonder if I'm tryin to come back home, to where I started, wonder if that's in my head, travelin at large. As a traveler with the Show, in my cheap wagon—have I ever told you about my Show Wagon? I'll have to tell you sometime. I said why the iron bars on my wagon windows Señor Shanks, why the big lock on my door, is this wagon for Heracles the old lion *feroz* for God's sakes? You wan to get raped or beat up some night? said Shanks. Some nights it's a thought, I murmured. Shanks riled. Bars on Heracles's wagon, he riled, is to keep him *in,* on yours to keep them *out.* Well one way *not* to keep em out is to make it look like a whore wagon, I said to Shanks. All the glass jewels of rubies and sapphires, tin moons and golden leaf paint. Yet a hovel inside. *Course* you don wan em in my wagon, see a pig sty, gold leaf and glass jewels on the outside, broken bed inside and roaches that travel as if twere part of the Show. We'll fix the bed, Shanks riled, we'll fix it I keep tellin you. You keep tellin me, I answered. People see glass and tin shinin for a mile away in the bright sunshine, see what you'd think was gypsy whores movin in the night, sparklin under the moon. No wonder they stoned it that time outside of Hannibal Missoura. Is why we have on the lock and iron bars, like I've told told you, says Shanks, gettin hysterical. You could not win with Shanks (nor could those bars keep *him* out when he'd had a few rums and Cokes, I can tell you, you wan hear?). As a traveler with the Show I was in almost every town and city of this old nation. This was in the nineteen hundred and thirties and the nineteen hundred and forties and the nineteen hundred and fifties. I believe the time of my excape, of becoming at large, was in the nineteen hundred and sixties, *no tengo por seguro*. I am not for sure. I know that right now as I sing to you it is in the nineteen hundred and seventies, near the end, it may be nineteen hundred and eighty I don know, nobody comes up to me and says what year it is. I only know that this old world is wearing out. I sing a sweet *adiós* to it. *Cantando, compadre. Canto*. You wan hear.

4

Come Back to
the Show

IT COULD BE SAID that I have run away from the Show. The word excaped was used by some, I'm sure. Oh they looked for me. That Tarrance Shanks surely shined his light in the bushes. One night right after I departed—which is a smart word for somebody crawling like a snake one minute then changin into a bat outta Hell the next—I saw fires in the darkness. They was ahuntin me in the bottomlands. Twas that Tarrance Shanks, my boss and head of the Show, leading a ridiculous posse. Composed of the Mescan Dwarft Eddy Gonzales my friend, powerful as a bulldog, *fuerte*, but with qualities of beautiful friendship, Josie Ella, the xylophone player, sweet but who had such a temper bent the keys of the xylophone with her little hammer, would beat with such fury sometimes, and my friend; but God help you if she came after you with her little felt-tipped hammer, would sting your brains out, *compadre*, felt tip had the sting of a wasp, Josie Ella said twas only shammy skin, I said twas made of thorns, give you an idea of what *Jesucristo* felt. And the dog Junipero Perro, a sweet white Mescan jumping dog that loved me always slept beside my side. We spoke Mescan together—course he didn't speak but when he barked to me so pertly he was speaking Mescan, for sure, *compadre.* They hunted me with affection—even that Shanks, for whom I was a valuable asset. Yet I bet they'd have killed me if they'd have had to, to keep me from excaping the Show, from leaving them. We used to speak about the world outside with vows to stick together forever. They hunted me with love and murder in their hearts. They come so close. Once Junipero Perro, silver in the dark, put his sweet nose to my brow where I crouched under a palmetto and I muttered *Te amo, Junipero, pero vate perro, go! vate perrito, dame la vida! A Dios!* A narrow excape! For a moment he gave me his warm tongue. But Junipero Perro did not rat on me, though I know his heart was confused and broken. A broken dog's heart! I suppose there's little worse than the broken heart of a dog, don you? I credit a sweet little white Mescan jumping dog for my successful excape to freedom—God's helper. That was a long time ago, that little dog is dust. Yet I miss the Show. I may go back, I don know. I don even know which town it's in. For the time being I am *at large.*

A recurring impulse to seek *noticias de mi madre,* some notice of her, recently recurred again and I am on the road ahuntin. I run out with that hunger and begun to look for her again. I had been living in a burnt-out kiln of an old sawmill, vines had grown all over it and had made of it a cool dark place. A couple of goats lived with me, billy and nanny, and twas peaceful. In the early mornings I heard the meadowlarks asinging. I guess folks knew I lived out there, outside of town where once twas a thriving sawmill, but nobody bothered me. When I went into the town and asked for anything to eat they give me some. Nobody was afraid and give me some. Once again I had that craving for *noticias de mi madre*. I will soon to tell you why, *oyente*, listener.

I had had a feeling that my mother Chupa met an early death. People like my mother Chupa run down fast like a flashing firework you see abursting on the ground at Fourth of July Fiesta: something crazy shoots it here, there, then it's out. But I don know, *compadre*, I thought as I went hunting for my mother Chupa that if I found her don know what I'd do, some days felt like I might choke her throat, what she done to me.

5

Chupa

A WOMAN OF WORN beauty had kept comin to the Show. Her beauty was wearing out on her—and so was the dress she wore, a green dress of thinning fringe, diamond-tipped, a tiny shining drip hung from the strings of fringe. I first noticed her on a Saturday night, a crowded night and a rainy night. My God the rain comin down on the Show. Mud on the shoes of my gazers and the smell of wet sawdust, the smell of the wet tent. There she was. Winkin green fringe, bruised green shoes with spangled buckles, tinsel combs in black long hair. Twas in Memphis, Tennessee. Come away, she whispered. Come with your mother, *su madre. Hijo hijito!* my little son! she whispered. I flared as though she had struck me like a match. Who are you, woman? I gnashed through my teeth. Did you get enough of wherever you've been? Are you through with whoever you've been away with? And now coming back to me? *Madre? Mamá?*

I saw her fall to her knees. Through a split in the crimson curtain of velvet that half circled me I saw her pray before me sitting in my gilded chair. I saw the pore glitter in her hair. I held still in my stillness of the Show, sitting in my gilded chair, looking straight ahead. But when one of my eyes fell again upon her I saw her mouth red as a plum murmuring, Midnight. Train depot. I had had other such offers. I held my stillness of the Show.

At midnight, as a Cowboy, *un Charro* under a wide sombrero and with a red sweat handkerchief around my throat like the Mescans working on the railroad wear, my ancestors, I was at the train depot, in the darkness of under the water tower. Paying no attention to my *Charro*, I could have been a Priest just as well, or God knows a redheaded woman, Chupa opened her ruby mouth to start talking and I said, I don wan hear it. She pouted and flounced her sparkled fringe and burred out a hot Mescan word. Let's get outa town, I said.

We left town together, a *Charro* and a *Puta*, my God, and went out a ways on the road towards the moon that seemed like was a white flake something was eating out a piece of, something was eating the moon. I wanted to choke my mother and wanted to lie on her breast. In the green light of the eaten moon I saw the figure of this woman smartin along on high heels, poppin up silver shiners, dartin white eyes, sparklings in her black hair, silver flurries all over, quiverin and poppin in flurries and little burstings; and I thought, what will douse her, what will flash out all this light from her, all this restless blink of her why won't she go out, what'll quench her? Mean but waiting for me to make one move of welcome, one reach of tenderness, pitiful, too, recently beautiful, young face, as if only this morning it had creased there around the mouth and only last night that skin there under her chin had slipped a little. She's beautiful, I thought, in her dancin starry fringe and her plump breasts under the dancin fringe and that black hair over her shoulders; and more alone than anybody in this world, gay and sparkling prancin though she was, cut away from everybody by her own hands, cut adrift *solitaria* by her own hands, just won't be tied to anybody or anything, think they have you then you leave em holding strings in their hand, a sparkle, you're gone, woman; cut away even from her own flesh and blood. So now you're back, intrudin onto me, what for? How long will you be here madam *Madrecita?* Looking good, anything I can do for you? Would you like a drink? Some coffee; gin? Are you hungry, *Tempestá?* When did you eat; need a little money? So the law is after you again? How long can you stay, Sweetheart, whore? *Corazón.*

When can we talk, she asked me. I wouldn't answer. When we could talk, arriving at an empty place in the woods by the river, we did not talk. We slept, tired to death, in each other's arms. Once I come a little awake, aswayin as if in a soft boat and twas my *madre* rockin me in her arms very softly in her sleep; I was in the nest of her, hair and feather strands; and smelt the smell of my mother; and once I come straight awake and in the white moonlight saw that face, saw it as familiar a feature as my own hand, saw a look before me that was ancient, old as my own eyes, the first image I ever in my life seen when my new eyes could gather vision and see—an ancient image of tenderness and craving, fear and awe and murder: my mother, the woman who bore me; and wanted right then to kill her, at the throat, with my hands; or lie upon her breast to go for her with my mouth, to suck her, my being was in my mouth, like in a fish; she drew me by my mouth, as in the very beginning. Lyin on her breast I felt *entero.* I was *total,* one. She had not known my division. Should I reveal myself to her? Reveal! The old word for the Show. Arcadio will not consent to reveal his final mystery to anyone. He has chosen to keep it a secret. Would she, like so many others, then flee me? Not my mother. She would see that I carried on my body herself and her man's self, my father's. That I was the walking replica of the two of them. A combination. I not only understood the nature of them both, I *was* them both. They had no secrets from me. This time my mother would not leave and she would not ever leave me again. When I chose to "reveal." Ladies and gentlemen Arcadio will now consent to reveal his final mystery. To his own mother! It was my trump card, my secret weapon, my instrument of vengeance.

But I heard a dog and I heard footbeats crushing through the vines. I crawled off fast and got into a big tight bush wound like a ball of baling wire and curled up in the very center. This is where I have told you the sweet Junipero Perro come to touch me farewell with his warm tongue. I don know where Chupa went or how she hid herself; but don worry they didn't find her. She could vanish under a flat rock, slide like a snake. A supreme disappearing act was my mother, the gypsy, the tramp, the runaway bitch left me behind long ago, just couldn't stay with anybody or anything, not even her own, always had to leave something, even a piece of her own body, an artist of magical vanishment, now you saw her now you didn't, not for half your lifetime you didn't, not for half your lifetime. What were you afraid of, bitch mother, Chupa, *mi madre, Madrequerida?* I cried out to myself God deliver me of this rage on my mother! *Oh I miss the Show and I may go back. I don know.*

In a little while it was all quiet again, my hunters

had gone, my darling Perrito had not ratted on me, and I emerged from the ball of weed my hiding place. No trace of *mi madre*. Gone again, I said. But in a moment more my eyes saw a dark figure and twas the woman herself. It was pitch midnight; no moonlight sparkled her. I swear to God she'd know how to turn off the moon if she had to, if moon shone on her and led somebody to find and catch her. She come to me. Lay down again, she said. My son. On your mother's breast and sleep. Tell me what you've done, I sternly said. I wan no more sleep till I hear what you've done. They was looking for you, not your mother, she answered. Because I excaped. For you, I snarled. Tell me your story of what you did, where you've been, I demanded quietly. Or I'll never lay on your breast again. What happened? *Madre mia, mi madre.*

6

The White Bible

UT BEFORE I TELL you my mother Chupa's story as she told it to me, I want to interrupt, or interfere, is that the word, something wonderful that come to me. I come upon a wondrous book with wondrous stories I keep tellin ever since I read them. Twas a little Mescan Bible fresh white when twas handed long ago to me as I sat in the gazing Show. A hand reached out to me and handed it to me. I could not see the face whose was that face that give the wondrous book to me—who was it oh who was it? In my glass jewel wagon I read the wondrous stories, of course tis yellowed now with the years and with handlin and from bein in the inside of my pocket where it rests to this day against my flesh when I'm not readin it, the little white Mescan Bible, I do not know the person who handed me the White Bible written in Mescan and never saw the face, who was it oh who was it; but the hand that reached out the white book to me handed me out my feelings of life, and my salvation, and many words, just the most wonderful stories in the whole world, though I had not read any other book ever in my life I know that this is so. But to tell the truth I never read a word until the hand handed me *La Biblia Blanca,* oh I could tell some *palabras* words that the women taught me in the *China Boy* but I never had much time to read even if I could, unless twas written on the flesh of a body. And I wrote ARCADIO my name. But to tell the truth I never read a word that twas not with the help of Eddy Gonzales the atheist Mescan Dwarft that did not believe in God. The nights in the chow tent and the nights in the glass wagon with the Dwarft areading me the stories was the starting of my life. I have not time to tell all the stories to you. I can tell you them almost as they was written down. Eddy was amazed that I could read em out almost exactly like they was written down and look up to the next page right on time, Dwarft said he was astounded. Guess I become a storyteller more than a reader.

I learned *también* from the tales outrageous that whores told, back in the *China Boy.* While other kids sat in school. A special one was a grand queen whore from Newark—said she was part Greek—and that her *madre* had been the principal of a school. Edna Pappas loved words more than anything. When she wasn't on her back she was reading a book—and even while she was, sometimes; she would crook around her head and study her ceiling, even though it jumped sometimes when her customer john was abouncing. When she said to him easy mister it was because he was interfering with her reading. The johns didn't know that she wrote on the ceiling over her bed the words that she was learning for that week, printed in *grande* letters. Every week she printed out a new list, her big ass up on a ladder while I held it. Oh we had fun. If a john shifted positions and looked up, what he might see if he held his eyes open would be a big word, like AD-MIR-ABLE or PRO-CRAS-TI-NATE. These are only a few of Edna Pappases words and some which I learned, among many others. Edna Pappas was improving herself for when she would one day get out of the *China Boy*. I wanted to do the same: the telling of tales *fantásticos* was what I wanted and the using of *grande* words, *palabras.* But for a long time I got off on the wrong track into a Show where I could not use my words but have to sit like a dumb ox, as you know, *Oyente,* but still—what I learned from Edna Pappas—I put my secret study words on a big boxtop down in front of me and nobody ever knew that I was learning them, I didn't even move my lips when I practiced them; sometimes if I did mouth a word the gazers thought I was apraying or talking to myself like a crazy person, when all I was doing was saying a divided-up word like Edna Pappas showed me to, *sílabas,* syllables. In this way I was getting myself ready for the world, to tell tales, *la grandeza* is what I wanted, *la extrañeza, la belleza,* you wan hear? My teachers I will always thank, one taught me from the ceiling of a whorehouse, one from a Bible, and one to tell tales *fantásticos* with tongue of tin or silver. Once I excaped, as you well know, *Oyente,* I used what was taught to me, the telling of tales and the using of words. I have talked off my head—which is a peculiar espression, if you wan think about it, to talk off a head. Edna Pappases brother Silvestro Pappas came almost every day to have a beautiful poet's conversation with his sister when she wasn't on her back, Silvestro Pappas was a poet, full of some bullshit but his tongue was a silver *angel's* tongue and a liar's tin one, too, and a bitter one, and *suave* and mean—*demonio*—but he told tales *fantásticos.* I listened and I learned *un poco* how to speak like Silvestro Pappas and to get the rough *Mejicano* sound of my ancestors out of my mouth, I wanted to speak big *habla*, to be *suave* in my speaking like Silvestro Pappas and to have the words like his sister Edna. I will tell, he said, you cocksuckers, about the five trees in a hidden canyon of Montana which remain undisturbed summer and winter and whose leaves do not fall. Whoever sees them will not experience death. I, Arcadio, have memorized this, do you hear how good is my *habla*, *Oyente*, do you hear how good is my *grande* speaking, just as I have learned by my heart the stories to read in *La Biblia Blanca*. Edna Pappas said him you will take me there to those trees when I have one thousand dollars in my sock. Unless, said Silvestro to his sister, you will have grown so old. That's why, answered Edna Pappas, I have to work very hard and with only rich johns. But Edna Pappas never got out of the *China Boy* to go to Montana to the hidden five trees, you wan hear? She waited too long. I used to tell her you better go now Edna Pappas and not PRO-CRAS-TI-NATE, but she kept waiting. I need one thousand dollars in my sock before I go, she said. But in a fight with her own brother she was stabbed by him under her tongue in her throat. Shut up! Silvestro yelled. Stop your goddamned words! Edna Pappases words was not stopped, though, but stayed on the ceiling because no one ever knew they was there but me. She was in the M's at the time of her stabbing. This was the immortality of Edna Pappas—*palabras grandiosas* on the ceiling of the *China Boy*, in a house of whores on a whore wharf.

When the white book was handed to me I went with it to Eddy and said what is this book? The Bible said he. The word written down of God. Show me how to read it I said. Eddy was not courteous to do it and besides since he was *un ateo* atheist; but I said you are my friend how did you read who learned you how to read? And Eddy said what good did it do me? *Por favor* Eddy I says, for your mother's sake. Her? said Eddy. Eddy was so bitter at everything. But he loved me and I give him the promise of tenderness, to touch me sometime because I knew how lonesome the pore Dwarft was and how he loved me, and because he could read. As a swap for reading out to me I let him handle me. Eddy was a hot little lonely Dwarft and I loved God and wanted to read his words. That was the bargain.

Our first lesson went sweet and I listened to the Dwarft read right out about the making of the world, of the moon and of the stars and waters. His little goose voice. He was surprising gentle when we studied reading together, surprising sweet and did have *la paciencia.* But he would not believe the stories of the book, he said. Why you hate God so much? I asked him. God is *posiblemente* a Dwarft, had you ever thought? Eddy Gonzales laughed so much and rolled like a clown and rocked his big head in his little hands and then stopped quiet and said, and maybe He is a half-man half-woman, and rolled and laughed and rocked his big head some more; and when he stopped I says, maybe. What's so fuckin funny?

At night when the Show was through and I was alone in my wagon with Junipero Perro the sweet white Mescan jumping dog, I told out from my *Biblia Blanca* as if I was areading it. I got *más y más* astounded, more and more. Junipero Perro was a very quiet *oyente* listener. God may be a white Mescan jumping dog, I says to him. And as the Show rode all day on the road toward another town, I told out from the white book like Eddy had read it to me. Sometimes I read out from it to my friends Eddy and Josie Ella in the chow tent, but of course not the old Shanks. Sometimes they intently listened, sometimes they was restless. I told them they could never set still like I had to in the Show. You jump and roll all over, I told Eddy the Dwarft, you don know about staying still; and you, I said, Josie Ella, you thrash and fling at your xylophone. I have to stay still, in the gazing stillness. Now let me read out and let me make some sound from my throat, for God's sake, I am not a *mudo* I have a tongue and can speak. But Eddy the Dwarft answered to me tell it in church I am an atheist why would I want to believe in a God that made a Dwarft with one of his hands like the fin of a fuckin fish? Well I says this is God's world and he hath made it, this white book has told me so and in Mescan so He made the Mescans too and He made the combinations and mixtures, *mestizos* of a dark and secret kind. Why not the Dwarfts? You got a better thing, said Eddy. Of *course* you can praise God and read out of the Bible. I drag my butt on the ground when I walk and have a fish's fin for a goddam hand. And my friend Josie Ella was *igualmente* not interested. She was a plain woman—when she took off the silvery wig—that sewed at night in the kitchen tent after the Show, drinking black coffee. She did not want to go to sleep for fear that her hands would harden. Besides she said Flora the lady cook that shared her wagon smelt of Irish potatoes. But once when she put too much brandy in the black coffee she told me that the reason she would not sleep was because she was afraid to die. She slept in cat sleeps in the kitchen sittin up. As long as I knew Josie Ella she had not finished somethin she was sewing on, she made so many mistakes and had to unravel. But she told us that she had to keep her hands movin all the time could not let them harden, for the xylophone of the Show; yet she made many a mistake and Shanks cursed at her and said twas because of all the black coffee and no sleep on her back, pore Josie Ella had her problems, too, like the rest of all of us.

Some of the wondrous things that I read out was about the big lions standing back from Daniel and did not bite or eat him, can you believe it, *amigo?* God sent an angel that shut the lions' mouths. The *feroz* lions was so impressed with the *angel* that they looked upon him with gentleness. Look there in the book and you will read it, *Oyente,* listener, you will see. *La Biblia dice que sí.* I said this to Emperor Colombo the "Lion Tamer" (ha! I have to laugh) that worked in the Show with old Heracles I told this wondrous story to him and Emperor Colombo said I don't give a shit. And oh of the proud King that ate grass for seven years. Says that his body was wet with dew of the grass and his hair grew long as eagle's feathers and his nails, the King's nails, was like birds' claws. *El rey orgulloso,* the proud King become a beast of the field and ate grass with the oxen, for his nasty pride. If you don believe me look in there, in *La Biblia* and you'll see it, what I'm tellin, you'll read it, *amigo, La Biblia dice que sí.* The Bible says so. *Pero* some do not believe. Unless, they say, I can see in his hands the print of the nails, I will not believe, see *los manos perforados con clavos* and put my finger into the print of the nails, I will not believe, and thrust my hand into his side, into *el costado perforado con lanzas,* with the swords his side was cut open, I will not believe (John 20:24). Well, then, behold my hands, says *Jesucristo;* reach out your finger and touch my hands; and reach hither thy hand and thrust it into my side, he said in the book. Because you've seen me, now you believe. But blessed are they that have *not* seen and yet believe, *Mire los manos perforados con clavos, mire los pies perforados con clavos, mire el costado perforado con lanzas, mire el frente perforado con espinas. Mire el cuerpo de Jesucristo.* Here is the body of Jesus Christ.

And says that there was once upon a time a stranger that nobody knew come into a rich town and nobody would give him any *hospitalidad,* closed their door on him when he knocked and asked for hospitality. *Finalmente* some poor people that were thrown out by the rich and selfish town that would not give welcome to strange visitors, *por ultimo* these poor outcasts of the *barrio* took him in and give him shelter. And in the middle of the night twas a terrible earthquake and storm of fire and when the poor people run to where the strange guest was sleeping they saw that he was a beautiful *angel* and the *angel* said do not have fear but follow me out of this damned town of *inhospitalidad* which is going to be blown up and burned down because of its sin of *inhospitalidad.* And they followed out the *angel* from the town to the top of a hill and heard a great esplosion and turned and looked down upon the town burnin and blowin up to destruction. If you do not believe this story, look there, in the Bible, and you'll see it, what I'm tellin you, you'll read it. Be kind to strangers and take them in and do not turn away strangers who knock on your door and give them somethin to eat if they ask for it and give them shelter, they may be a very *angel. La Biblia, La Biblia Blanca dice que sí.* So *compadre, Oyente,* if anybody does not welcome you, turn and go away from them and shake the dust of their house and of their town and of them off your feet and go on your path to where you are agoin. This is what the Bible tells us.

WILLIAM GOYEN

And if I could tell one more, about the pool of water
that the *angel* troubled and then it cured the affliction of
the afflicted; but that a paralyzed man laid there by the
pool for thirty-eight years waiting for this *angel* to move
the waters, waitin for the movin of the water. Because he
had no one to help him into the waters when they moved
and others pushed in front of him, this paralyzed man
never could get into the healing waters. When *Jesucristo*
come and heard this man's story he told him to just forget
trying to get into the water and just to get up and take his
cot and walk and not wait on the water. The man did this
and walked off with his cot, to his amazement. But the
policía of the town arrested him for carrying his bed in
the street on the Sabbath and then the man said but I've
been paralyzed on this cot for thirty-eight years and today
a man come and healed me up on my feet from this very
damned cot. Who is this man? the *policía* asked, and the
man said I don know, he left. Tell it to the judge, the
policía said and led the once-paralyzed man on off,
awalking, towards the judge. But then they saw a man
acomin and it was the man and the once-paralyzed man
said yonder he is that's the one, and when the *policía*
asked the man if he was the one and he said yes and they
said what is your name the man said *Jesucristo*, this man
has been forgiven of his sins and now walks, let him
alone. And to the man he said go on, now, you are free,
and be of help to others. And finally to *la policía* he said
the spirit heals but the letter killeth. I do not know esactly
what that means but I get the gist. But you can read it in
the book I'm tellin you about, this is what the Bible says,
La Biblia dice que sí, that Eddy Gonzales the Mescan
Dwarft learned me to tell out of, almost as if I was areading it.

ARCADIO

35

7

My Mother Chupa's Song, Interrupted by a Little of Mine

NOW TO GET BACK TO where I left off, to tell my mother's story as twas told by her to me on the night of my excape. Chupa said that she run away from my father Hombre crazy from his drunkenness and his mean violence on her. One night said she just run crazy out the door into the night, didn't know where, didn't care. My father tore her dress off her back trying to keep her but my mother Chupa run on. She run down the dark road and stopped by a pond and climbed up into a tree and curled in there to hide in the deep tree, and said she heard all night the terrible sobbing of the bullfrogs in the pond. Because she loved my *papá* Hombre, she said, and always would. He was a man nobody could ever leave, just get away from. I've never let him go in my heart but had to get away, big sonafobitch *cabrón* tearing me to pieces and biting at my neck like a big snake. I felt like a big snake had a hold of me, she told me. I ought to know what kind of a snake he was, I said. Maybe I'll tell you *my* story of him. Lived with him longer than you did. What else could I do? Chupa asked me from so deep in her throat I couldn't almost hear her.

Su padre era un hombre bárbaro, made you on me when was *loco* from uppers and beer. Where was it? I wanted to know. The room was in a Texas river town in a rayroad boardinghouse, I was a bride. That's where your father Hombre made you on me. *Loco* on me, a wonder I didn't get you in my throat. That's all he wanted from me, I begun soon to see that. Five years he punched babies into me and I didn't hold them in me, three babies I didn't hold from him before I run away. But you stayed, I kept you inside me. A lotta good it did me, I said, that you kept me inside of you, you left me, you didn't take me with you, I scowled her. Wished you didn't hold me like those other three you didn't keep inside you that was the way I felt a long long time *mi madre* but now I've changed, where have you been in all the long meantime since you kept me inside of you? Said she was in lots of towns, New Orleans, Shrevesport, El Paso, Memphis, Napa, California. I don wan hear the towns, I said. But what would two have done on the roads and in the towns if one could hardly make it—and one of them a little kid of five? *Mi madre* esplained to me. How would I know? I shrugged.

Who are our kinfolks among the Mescans I asked *mi madre* who was your Mescan *madre* who was your *padre? Indios* she said and I said what is that what is an *Indio?* Old people of the race, said *mi madre. La Raza. Los Antiguos* that was told to me by *mi abuela* my old grandmother Lupe Luisa. Said *La Raza* the race *es muy antigua.* Would not die nobody could wipe them out, said *mi madre.* Once the whole *raza* was eaten up by coyotes. Next time a great huge wind blew all *La Raza* away, and then next rain of fire and next flood of great water. But we went on, *los Indios.* This is what my grandmother told me about us Mescans Chupa said. I do not know any more except that the *Españoles* Spaniards cut off the head of my grandmother's grandfather when my grandmother was a little girl and put it in a cage and hung it on the *plaza*. My mother's story made me feel very old and lost *perdido* is our word for it. Where are your mother and father, I asked Chupa. I do not know, she said. *Quién sabe? No me importa.* Would you like me to go with you to hunt for them? No, she said. What am I, I asked my mother. *Mestizo*, she told me. Mixed. Half and half. Are you *mestiza?* I asked Chupa *mi madre.* Pureblooded, she said. And do not ask more questions.

Because when *mi madre* Chupa run off *Papá* and I lived in a whorehouse over a Chinese restaurant by a dead river in Memphis, Tennessee, *China Boy* was name of it if you wan hear it, you wan hear it? Twas owned by a seventy-year-old fox name of Shuang Boy, not a bad man in hisself but a cutthroat woman dealer. Had the gist of sex like a hot fox, could deal in it as if twas canned tomatoes, was a crackerjack storekeeper, ace salesman of it— and I don mean canned tomatoes. That's somethin you cain't can. That's somethin you cain't can, or Shuang Boy would've, that Chinaman would've sold it in a can if could've. I was never sure what my *papá* did for Shuang Boy but I guess he was a kind of a strawboss of his women. My *papá* Hombre walked around naked with's can of beer in his hands is all I saw him do. I looked upon my father's nakedness. Whenever I asked him about *mi madre* he let go such a swearin that I'd hide under somethin until he cooled off. Then he'd say 'Cadio 'Cadio where have you gone? Commere you little sonofabitch, didn't mean to scare you away, commere I'll give you a ice-cold Coca-Cola, why you shiverin so? But all day I'd turn away from him and wouldn't say a word. I planned to run away, partly to be alone and to be away from him and partly to try and find my mother. But my *papá* had his good side to him and then he could be a sweet man, and gentle; blue man, though, blue and soft man when he wasn't drinkin. You wan hear it? *Mi padre* Hombre took me to buy me white shoes for Easter and took me to the vaudeville show at the *Memphis Sunshine* on a rainy Sunday afternoon where the bubblin colored lights bubbled in the Memphis rain, give me a feelin for runnin away to a place that would be like the colored bubbles in the rainy air of hot Memphis, Tennessee.

But when *Papá* drunk beer and walked up and down naked it was *terrible.* He was on the rampage and wouldn't stop until he wore himself down. Sometimes that took a long time. And I hid again to where he couldn't find me and made him call and call for me and look for me. And I would see him with the women. I would see what he did with them and scared me and give me feelins that I didn't want to have. Because I seen that what he did with the women was what he'd done with me; one time he caught me and pulled off all my clothes and I was revealed to him. From then on I would hide where he couldn't get to me up on top of the closet, when I saw him comin drunk and swingin his big member at me. When I was eleven and one of the women was ahuggin me and touched and took me down with her and found me there was when the whole thing started. I laid down with the women then and the men they had and my father too, more and more, in his drunkenness, and Shuang Boy, too, he was with me in his *calor* hotness and his old hot yellow lizard's body. But my father clung to me and held me close until he almost killed me with his green mad eye aburnin upon me, shiverin and crazy and callin my name and tellin me I was his, all his own and that we was savin our money to run away together. You wan hear it?

And they sold me in the *China Boy.* Everbody wanted me and it cost a lot. I never saw much light of day until I was fifteen. I laid in a shadow. My days was days of rollin *lujuria* lust in a shadow and my nights a half-darkness of hot juice and sweat and slippin flesh on mats and beds in rooms. I didn't care, I loved it. I guess I really wanted to die. You wan hear it, don you? *Oyente,* listener. You not gonna run away, *Oyente,* are you? You wan hear it don you? Once Shuang Boy sent me out on a week's hideout with a big oilman named Drake, big horny man but gentle like they are, a big rough tender man, out in the mesquite country on a ranch. That oilman offered me anything I wanted, the moon and stars, to stay with him, live back in the mesquite country on the hidden *rancho* with an old whiteheaded black woman to watch after me. Drake brought me purple silks and rosy satins and you won't believe it but a diamond chain so long it dropped its sparklin little stars of diamonds down upon my young breasts. But I said you forget the cowboy of me, the *charro* part, Señor. I am not all rosy satins and diamond chains. Give that to the women, he said. Give me a cowboy hat, I said, and some cowboy boots, give me a horse. And I stole out once and walked in his starry cowboy boots and an embroidered *sombrero* along a cold green flashin little deep river in heat of one hundred and two degrees out in the hidden country of mesquite, and felt my balls, the power of my balls, I was a strutting *charro,* felt lonesome and wanted to be on the prairies going along with a strong horse under me between my legs and was so mixed up then and thought who am I, what am I? And could have run then but I wasn't ready, I was fourteen I was not ready to give up the *China Boy*, all the flesh and hot hiding and all the feelins, the wild feelins I was a slave to, and people aloving me day and night. You wan hear it? Maybe you don wan hear this much, maybe you think I got a liar's tongue of tin in my head telling a tale *fantástico* that Silvestro Pappas taught me, but it is the truth I'm telling, tongue of silver, I'm singin the truth what happened to me. I could have run away many times, but I was a slave to my feelings, *esclavo* of flesh, couldn't quiet down couldn't give it up, slave of being wanted, and wanting the feelins, *esclavo* of being a special piece. I was an addict, I uz doped, crazed, I uz in a cyclone of sex I uz in a coma of sex, I uz drenched in it soaked in it, you wan hear it you wan hear it? Oh I may go back, I may go back to the Show, I just may, the life I've led. I may go back to the glass jewel wagon and the golden chair of silence and gazing, give up words give up the telling of tales *fantásticos* and the mouthing of words, give up *la grandeza* and *la belleza*, and speak no more.

One early morning I run out of Shuang Boy's. By dawn I was out of town in a cowboy's clothes. I was worn out and ashamed I was sick to death of my body and of my feelins, sleepin in the weeds outside of towns and cryin in the grass. One day outside of a town, because of my unbearable feelings, I tried to fix myself with a piece of glass but couldn't get the courage to do it—and to tell the honest truth I couldn't make up my mind which of myself to try and eliminate, I had no favorites, my life-long problem in that terrible night of dying in my soul *Jesucristo* come to me and told me to accept myself just as I was, that He had made me as He had made all things and would be my companion from then on, wherever I went if I would have Him. Oh Jesus *Jesucristo*, I said, are you like me? Like you, said *Jesucristo*; and in the morning in peace I got up out of the weeds of the field and started on my way of acceptance, wanderin and abeggin at back doors. Little did people know that *Jesucristo* was with me at their back door, knockin, and when they come to ask what I wanted and saw me hungry and heard me ask have you got anything to eat? they give me some bread and they was afeeding Jesus Christ our Lord. I'm only tellin you what happened. If you wan hear. That's all I'm singing you.

Oh twas people in cities still tried to pay me to do things, as of yore in the house of Shuang Boy, in the *China Boy*, to come to a hotel room and lay on a bed while they all looked and watched and drank, but I would not; and some rich men in Fort Worth offered me a whole lots of money to come away with them to a huntin lodge and let them all have a party with me. But I would not. Was the love of *Jesucristo* saved my soul and saved me from lecherousness, from just going down into the dirt for love of the flesh and the feelins and just not caring; *Jesucristo's* love kept me from feelin I was a freak, a Sideshow like Old Shanks called me, old bastard, and thrown back by the human race, give me some human dignity. Else I would have fallen low again cause of my special flesh I was born with and was put on me to test me, though I had temptations more *terrible* than could be told, and tis true that I had given in to all I told you when I was young and couldn't stop. Oh I did some things, have to admit, got off with the wrong people a few times and let em have their way. Twas because I was so lonesome and in my lonesomeness remembered those feelins from what Shuang Boy's house shown to my body, back there in those days I have described to you, in the *China Boy*. Such feelins come over me sometimes that I didn't know what to do, thank God they've all gone by the wayside, majority of em, and I got some peace from that hellfire of feelin come over me when I let them have their way. Twas from those hellfire of feelins that I almost lost my way. I would wake up naked in the moonlight laying hurtin and thinkin Lord God *Jesucristo* what's happenin to me am I bein stabbed am I bein stung am I goin to bust open what is drenchin me and burnin me and meltin me, I got all this on me, all this, and wish I'd never found out what it could do to me, what feelins it could give me, cause now I don know how to forget them, can't stop them, cause now I know and have been hurt crazy by these feelins and I can't get away from them now they have been laid heavy on me again, my God would make a lunatic out of me, a crazy hurtin gaspin thing out of me, cryin out for ease. Wish I could be a holy saint or a person without any feelins, a poor *idiota* like that Hector; or just a boy, a boy without the changin and hurtin that comes to you in a while, before you know it you done changed from something skippin along or off singin by yourself to a secret somethin lookin and huntin and wantin in the dark, lets you know what you got on you and the wild feelins that can come from what you got on you, wish I could go to a magician and have him wipe them off of me with a magic wand or with the wave of a silken handkerchief, or in a puff of smoke; or just paint over them as you can do on a picture. In me *Satanas* put on one body the two biggest troublemakers ever created from flesh onto one body and give that one person the torments of the whole human race, man and woman, all in one. Tis me. Arcadio. You wan hear.

And I kept on havin, from time to time, offers of a lots of money, from people who wished me to display the work of nature on my flesh; but I would not. And one time a Turkish man, a rich Turk, wanted me, to take me away and put me in a little palace all of my own. I don know what town but in some town in Turkey, I guess. Turkish man said he would put silks and satins on me and pearls and rubies and just possess me all his own forever, pleasin me in any and every way that I wanted. This, I must admit, was a proposition, for the Turk was a *muy caro* person and I had nothing, not one thing, twas a real temptation, for pleasure and pearls and a little palace—a little security. But I would never have any privacy and would be owned by someone. And I would be back into my hellfire. So I would not. I would not go with this Turk.

But the thing that really changed my life was that one night I come upon a Show travelin through Texas but pitched in a pasture outside of town of Refugio, a Mescan town of Texas, and the word come to me Investigate. So I went and said where's the boss and they told me and I found the boss, Old Shanks, Tarrance Shanks, and said to him that I wanted a job and Old Shanks said doing what, and we went out in the field and I showed myself to the man, revealed myself, *mi cuerpo*, and Shanks said Jesus Christ. And after a minute said do you have any talent? Well I can play a good waltz on the frenchharp—a little; "The Waltz of the Spotted Dog," I said. Never heard of the waltz but you got a job, said

Tarrance Shanks to me, and wondered would I show myself, "nature's harvest," completely revealed, on the side
to a special few who would no doubt be willing to pay an
added fee. They would be screened out to detect any
freaks who had abnormal ideas, man said. But I would
not. I just would not. What would be my salary, I wanted
to know. *Cinco* a week plus board and room, the man
Shanks said, using a Mescan word the way Texans do.
And I responded with a quick shot of Mescan, rattled out
such a quick bunch of Mescan that it stopped him dead
in his tracks and the man said what is that? And I said
tips. It means in Mescan any tips? We have a sign outside
says No Tips to the Attractions. That's general proce-
dure, said Tarrance Shanks.

Though it was not a very good offer I agreed to dress
up on the outside to indicate what's on the inside for an
additional one-fifty. But Shanks said not until there was
an increase in attendance. Business's been bad, he com-
plained. Said twas because of rain and taxes.

I took the job so I could always be among people,
even if twas just settin still and gazin while bein gazed at
and not bein alone in some faraway palace in Turkey or
some cheap hotel in some city. And time passed on until
where my mother Chupa found me and I excaped at her
suggestion.

I'd like to pull out a ragged photograph, once tinted
but now the tint is faded away in most spots, taken of me
in Albuquerque once when I was at my fullest. Perhaps
you will someday remember me. In it you will see me
wild-looking, something dangerous in my facial glance, in
my dark Mescan flashin face of burnin eyes and red lips
with some of the red still on them if you'll notice and my

black head of curling hair, tis a wondrous thing this photo and shows me how I was, if you don believe me now. Perhaps you will remember me. And while you gaze awhile upon it I will play my frenchharp, the waltz called "The Waltz of the Spotted Dog," my favorite through the years and the only song I know. You wan hear?

My Mother Chupa's
Song Continued

S O SAID SHE WAS
twenty-one when she run away from my father and me.
You wan hear it? With her dress torn off her back said she
run into the night, looking back to see a drunk man running crazy after her, falling and getting up and floun-
dering and running and falling, until she did not look
back any more. *Chupita!* she heard a voice cry. But my
mother did not look back and run on.

For some time she traveled in the company of a
blond man that was excaping the Law which was in pur-
suit of him. This man Joel had stolen enough money for
him and my mother Chupa to flee comfortably from city
to city, living in pretty good hotels and eating in good
cafés. Joel gambled and kept winning, my mother said.
But when he suddenly lost everything they had to live
with nothing in terrible places. My mother said she suffered bad from poverty. She was often dirty and hungry.
Which led her to despise herself, she said. The blond
man Joel wanted to rob a place but my mother would not
offer her help as an accomplice, dressed like a man as he
suggested and showing a revolver to a bank clerk. It was

somewhere in Sonoma County that the blond man Joel wanted to make this robbery, my mother remembered and told me. You want to ask which particular town I'm sure but please to hold your questions I like to tell my story in as much of one piece as I can, *por favor—chiquito.* The way you would not interrupt a singer and his song, *comprendes.* My mother Chupa would not lend her hand to a robbery. She would, however, agree to loiter nearby in an alley and wait for Joel to finish his deed. She was dumb enough to believe that he would come out of the bank like he was just another person who had cashed a small check and walk on calmly away with her—which was precisely his plan, according to what my mother Chupa told me. My opinion is that Chupa my mother should have cut herself away right then and there from Joel the blond man, given him the shake-off; but of course I see that the poor woman was in love with him and afraid to lose him, and afraid to be alone in the world, way up in the Valley of the Moon in Sonoma County California, God only knows which town, she never told me.

Of course they blew off the crown of Joel's blond head. And right before my mother's eyes while she stood in her appointed place looking in Joel's face as he come towards her. He fell at her feet and she fell upon him— and all the bank money that had fallen out—and held him to her. You've blown his brains out she screamed to the Police. Get out of the way lady, the Police shouted to her, you're cradling a dangerous criminal wanted over the entire Valley of the Moon. Well he's not wanted any more my mother said she said, as they pulled her up from the crownless Joel. In her bosom was a hundred-dollar bill and two twenties which she'd slipped there. Said she saw

Joel's blue eyes looking green at her through the red blood. Do you know this robber? the Police asked her. No, I'm in the nature of a Good Samaritan, said she told them. Then please go on your way, he's beyond any Good Samaritan, let go of him lady.

That's how my mother Chupa started the next piece of her life, bloodstained with a blond man's blood and with one hundred and forty dollars of stolen bank cash in her bosom in far up Sonoma County in the Valley of the Moon in California, I don know what town. Maybe Vallejo I don know even if it is in the Valley of the Moon or even if tis a town may be a valley, Vallejo is all she told me, Vallejo. My mother was afraid to try to use the one-hundred-dollar bill for fear of being suspicioned and so she kept it in her bosom. The forty dollars got her started with clean clothes and off on her own—to where? Where was she to go, where was my mother to go, so alone? With another man, of course. Who popped right up before the day was over. By nightfall he'd had his hand in her bosom and fingering the hundred-dollar bill. Senseless because a man had his fingers on the nipples of her breast, poor fool of lonesomeness and sex that my mother was, she lost the hundred-dollar bill in that manner, in the fashion that I have just told you.

Coming back to her senses she spied through the hotel window the man hurrying away on the street, and within a flash she was down after him and saw him enter a bar and run in and caught him as he lifted a premium beer to his red lips that recently put her momentarily into a blackout with their kisses. Why don we spend the hundred-dollar bill together, Señor, my mother said to him. Or I'll call the cops to throw your butt into the jail of this town you cheap swindler. Her eyes flashed fire at him,

I'm quite sure. Baby, said the man, whose name was Joe Schwartzman, what greater pleasure. I was just going to the phone to phone your room and invite you down for a drink at my courtesy. I'll show you courtesy, my mother said, and made as if to go for his throat. And in this way Joe Schwartzman and my mother joined up together. They had each other's number right from the start. A gentle blond robber whose piece of head was blown off the size of a Yarmulke, whose piece of head was dropped like a Yarmulke into my mother's lap, provided Chupa with the means—a hundred-dollar bill—to discover a dark Jewish lover. Life is truly an unusual journey, *verdad? Un viaje maravilloso.* A crazy trip that ofttimes knows not its own name and we forget we are in the hands of God.

———

Joe Schwartzman was a hot young Jew with good lips who knew how to blackout a woman with lip sucks and tongue lickings. My mother Chupa said never before or after had she ever known such a sex and heat as resided in Joe Schwartzman's fingers lips and sexual member— not to mention his horned tongue, said Joe Schwartzman had a little horn on the end of his tongue. My God, revolting, I cried. You try it you'll see, my mother said. Well it's a dead man's tongue now, so why argue, I told her. And said that Joe Schwartzman had the combination wordflow of a brilliant college professor and a door-to-door salve salesman—a man of such persuasion could convince you that *Jesucristo* was a redheaded woman. He was on the road with Lorco Products, a drummer from town to town of pretty kitchen things. He would give demonstrations in women's homes and, in a kind of a show, sell these women Lorco Products. My mother said she didn't have to mention what she imagined Joe Schwartzman offered—and awarded when he could—as fringed benefits to the women. God knows, she said, women in small towns. Not to mention Joe Schwartzman in a house full of women in a small—or big, for that matter—town. But she had the one hundred dollars on him and it was his debt of this big bill to her that—she honestly said she believed—kept his horned tongue back of his teeth *most* of the time, kept him from any monkey business and true to her—*most* of the time, she said.

Talk about a talker, my mother Chupa talking could charm a rattlesnake to rattle *La Paloma.* Wait a minute I sometimes had to say, Chupita, could we have a moment's silence? *Que tienes, muchachito?* she'd ask. You sick? *Chico chiquito!* And she'd grab me to her and clutch me. *Que tienes? Que tienes?* Shhhh, she'd whisper, shhhh, as though *I* was the one to be quietened, and gently rock me. Why did I cry when she rocked me, why did I cry upon that breast of my mother that I'd sought all these years in so many places, cursing her with my vile tongue—that breast that smelled of my mother's smell which had been captured in my nose for my lifetime, only my mother had that smell in her breast that's what I'd been waiting for, *madre sagrada, madre diabolica, madre mia.*

Anyway, my mother Chupa told me that Joe Schwartzman had sold his last dishpan the day he met her, though he did not yet know this—nor did she. For on that very midnight she found him making love to a local housewife, standing up, in the corner of a parking lot and stabbed him in the back on his forward movement, said the reflex of his muscles went on after she sunk into his lung the blade of a knife she carried against treachery and his cry of death was his cry of love, two stabbings one of love and one of death; and the housewife fell over onto his face-up body still hunching and wriggling and my wicked mother Chupa said to him, better get it quick it's goin to be your last one and said the housewife leapt up and went crazed and ran around the parking lot howling in the dark. My mother confessed this killing to me and her teeth gnashed white in the darkness with an old vicious jealousy, but her tears dropped hot on me when she told that she was never apprehended by the authorities, but God apprehended me, she told me, God caught me and only He knows my debt, God knows; and she my mother Chupa was a heaving vessel of mixed feelings and sank into her lightless fringe like a musty hen, both wanting my sympathy and daring me to give it to her. I let my mother alone until she struggled through the tempest of her feelings. After which she chanted a long bunch of words in the Mescan speech of her forefathers and which translated told me that I had a half brother in this world somewhere, given her by Joe Schwartzman's wild loving on the only day she knew him and born of her, under evil airs of murder and guilt and suffering, nine months later in a jail in Missoura where she had been locked up seven months pregnant not for the crime of killing but for stealing the green-fringed, diamond-tipped dress that hid her seven-months child; under a swaddle cover of soft fringe and silver shiners this child swelled up his mother and mine until he burst out of her in her cell of the Missoura jail—she never told what town—to the surprise of the jailer and the judge, an old drunken fool with a harelip but he let her go free, she said; *mi madre* brought this bursting child out of her with her own hands, in secret in the night. The name of my brother that my mother gave him when he was born was Tomasso. She left Tomasso in the Missoura jailhouse for adoption and he was brought up in a Missoura jailhouse in an unnamed town adopted by the jailer and his wife. My God, I called, I have somewhere a brother. And you have a dead Jewish stepfather, stop grieving over completely lost things she told me, stop taking everything I tell you so hard, I want to forget it all. But my half-brother Tomasso is not lost, I said, and for God's sake who are *you* to tell me to stop taking everything so hard. And besides I am not taking it so hard I am only listening attentively as I have been accustomed to for years in the Show. But now I will have to begin to wonder how to find Tomasso. Why don't you look in Missoura? Chupa asked me. Because I am sure he has excaped by now, I says to her. And anyways, where is Missoura? Don't ask me, Chupa said. I was only in jail in it. How do you know that Tomasso is not dead like his Jewish father and besides how many can you look for, father, half brother, mother? Well, I found you, I told my crazy mother. Who answered I found *you*. In a Sideshow. It was my home, I spat back; something *you* never gave me. It was a Show, she spat at me. For deformities. Fake deformities. What is this world, I cried out, *what in damnation is this world?* It was not an *act*, I said, pulling back from what was going to be a fight between us. It was a cheap act and one to humiliate your mother, my mother shouted, until I came to get you out, and I shouted, it was not an act! And she cried humiliation! Cheap humiliation she screamed from a face that was wild with her feelings of fear and self-hate and run off a ways and turned her face from me and cried into her hands, bitterly and for herself, for all her life that she had just told me—and for more than I could know, but not for me. And while she sobbed her lonesome anguish, cut away, again, from the world, and by her own hands had done it, again, cut herself away, with one hand, you wan hear it, I opened my pants and with both hands pulled down my pants to my ankles and lay back. *Look*, I said softly, *Mama look*, I said softly with softness and love, without blame or anger, I don know why it wasn't anger but I guess because it was the work of God, I said *Mama look*. I am revealed. My mother turned, whimpering, and gazed upon me lying revealed in the firelight; and then she came closer and looked down upon me and then my mother Chupa stepped back from me, and back, stepped back whispering *O Dios O Dios O Dios* and vanished into the trees, someplace way back, and the night was silent, where was my mother was she praying was she going to steal back and kill me? And then I heard her crying. Mama, I called, why you cryin; don cry for me. I already cried enough, God knows, tears enough to fill a hundred buckets. Nobody ever cried for me but me and tears enough I've cried to fill a bowl to wash your long black hair; don cry for me. There was no answer. And I laid on there, as alone as ever; quiet, though, now; and finally revealed the final mystery; the final mystery that Old Shanks could never get from me in the Show; and now felt older and more of myself, don know why exactly; and laid on, laid on awake and under the eternal stars, naked as God made me and revealed to Him; and the night passed. You wan hear it.

At daybreak I built a fire, and my mother Chupa come back, smelling the fire. We was quiet and then I said to her quietly, and loving her, what'd you expect, the

Dallas Morning News? And then to my surprise I felt myself breaking into crying, so full, for the whole story of my mother, and for my whole story, all what happened to me, for the whole troubled thing, our lives, that just suddenly drownded me down like heavy water over me. Then my mother swept like a wave of water into her sobbing and we cried deep and full together, *lágrimas de dolor lágrimas dolorosas, negro es el color de nuestras tristezas,* like the Mescan song says. I'm sorry for your black life of shit, I told my mother, rubbing off tears with the back of my hand for some reason laughing now.

I've had some good of it, I heard her say while she begun to comb down her black bitter hair.

Don you think I haven't out of mine? I said. *Corazón* . . . ? Sweetheart?

You seem to be getting ready to go someplace? I asked, sensing the old abandonment, the way she used to brush her hair before she went out.

To relieve myself, she said.

I never saw my mother Chupa again. You wan hear it? Twas later said to me by somebody that twas the sin of uncovering, of revealing, that put a curse on my mother Chupa—or another one, seems to me, she was born already with a curse—as in the White Bible when Noah was looked upon uncovered and a curse fell upon the viewer of his nakedness—his very son. Sent my mother wandering away, the uncovering of my nakedness. God knows, I don't. But although I will be telling you of hunts for her and espectations of her you might as well know now that never again did I find my mother Chupa. That morning by the fire I waited and waited long after the fire had sunken into ashes and cold. But *mi madre* Chupa never did come back to me. To relieve herself indeed, well she relieved herself that morning, relieved herself of me forever. That was her swan song with me, though I did not know it then.

Since it was my mother cause me to excape from the Show to meet her then run away from me again, I decided to remain excaped and search for Tomasso who had swollen up my mother and burst out of her in a jail in Missoura, I do not even know which town. In searching for my half brother, I might just come upon my mother Chupa now excaped from me; and, who knew, might even come upon my father Hombre somewhere, running his long member up somebody; or sitting blue and old somewhere with a bottle of beer. Maybe I could bring us all together.

More of
La Biblia Blanca

HUNTED THEN Tomasso. But some feeling rises up into my head from the old White Bible to tell you about. Did you know about the time they were fishing, right after *Jesucristo* had been crucified some of his disciples was afishing, and a stranger on the shore called out to them have you got anything to eat? *Tiene algo de comer?* Well this rises up out of *La Biblia* to me. When one of the fishermen saw who it was he was so excited that he jumped out of the boat and run through the water to him. Twas Peter, *querido Pedro.* What love they had! How glad they were to see this friend that had been nailed and killed and put in the tomb and then come up to life only a few days before. That is a wondrous story about the beautiful man that was believed now to be dead, the very man that had already told these fishermen insomuch as you do it to the least of these you do it to me. Some days after they had killed him, *Jesucristo* come to the shore and asked for something to eat. I think *Jesucristo* is hungry, too, *compadre.* That he needs us all to feed him, too. Oh I would be very happy to give *Him* something to eat, and oh I think that probably I have given Him my whole body, that I have turned over my whole body of flesh to Him. That is, if He will have it. But I think, *amigo*, that if the Holy Spirit that I told you about cared so much about *el rey orgulloso* that ate grass, about Daniel among the *feroz* lions and about the paralyzed man that walked after thirty-eight years of paralysis and got arrested, and about oh so many others like you and me with holy wishes and wild feelings, I think, then, that that Holy Spirit, *Espíritu Santo*, would care as much for me, an older runaway at large in the world and looking for God and for his mother. Because you see, *Señor*, I live in a dangerous possibility of giving myself to myself, *comprendes?* Is possible. Sometimes in true love, tender and soft, other times, *Señor, Señora, Señorita*, in plain wild *chingando*, that is the word for it, *con permiso*, have to tell you that, have to be honest, have to tell you the truth. This is the possibility that always hovers over me. Flexo, the boneless acrobat in the Show, was able to kiss hisself, bent his body into a wheel of hisself and kissed it, Shanks charged extra for men to see it, but I'm not talking about that. *Comprendes?* You wan hear? If you was to lift my shirt you would find a sight, and I bet your feelings would be so mixed up that you would run away from me, too, like my mother Chupa did. Being all things in one, I was made self-sufficient. I am equipped for lust, just sitting down or standing in one place, tantalized by my own very body, sometimes itching and burning, sometimes soft open and hard, lip and cod, one part hungering for the other, and it available and welcoming and no hunt necessary, hunter and hunted I hunt myself, the hunt leads me no farther than the distance of a reach across my own body, what I seek in my maddened quest is at hand, a simple journey of my fingers, merely within grasp, yet I have gone almost *loco* in the game of it, the tricks and games, I became cunning, I became shifty and secret and coy and *macho* and *galán*. I was the battleground of myself I almost tore myself in two. I could go mad. I would get a streak going. When I used to get a streak going, look out. Then I was a common piece and got a streak in me, all connected to my wildness, wildness of words and wildness of feelings. And oh my *Jesucristo* sometimes wildness of action. Sometimes when I got a streak I didn't give one flying *chinga. Muñeco! Muñequito!* Little Mescan doll. Oho! That old name they tenderly called me in the days of yore; *Muñequito. Muñequito mejicano, bésame bésame bésame,* gimme a Mescan kiss. When my streak streaked through me seems like I flamed into something way beyond, listen to me listener *Oyente,* oh how then I loved to regard myself, to look at my beauty, revealed to myself, the extraordinary *miraglo* of myself, sometimes I looked and looked in that Show-gaze people used on me sitting still and perfect like a perfect statue or a perfect figure of wax, me perfect and still before the eyes of gazers in the perfect stillness of the Show, of being looked at, still, by still figures all struck still. Myself! A figure of wonder! How I love to turn that cold serene and intense gaze upon myself. And this self-looking, this glaring gaze turned upon myself, has given me a wisdom of the flesh, *chiquito,* given me a gift of soul in the flesh. For I was always in close touch with myself, you understand. I've had a long, deep association with myself. Only *I* know the long journey with myself that I have had, the untold life of me . . . which now I tell: I fulfill myself. My right side turns to my left. I couple. I unite myself. I am a wholeness whose parts have struggled with each other. I bear mortal enemies upon my person. I tease and seduce. I alone am a conversation of two heard in parks and alleys and doorways and upon beds, the ancient beg, the ancient refusal, *give it to me; no, not now, not yet.* Always there, it is not always available; my parts bargain; hot and bargaining they strive upon my body; I could go mad from the negotiation, be torn apart by the old negotiation, proud cock and subtle cunt working at the old negotiation. You wan hear, you wan hear? I know *them!* You wan hear? I got a very special knowledge. Almost as if I made them I know these two, I got a close acquaintance; like a watchmaker knows a watch I know their workings. Yet I have almost died in my knowledge of their workings, obsessed with myself, possessing myself long days on hidden beds, a tormented wheel, a howling acrobat, my body assailing my body, I have almost died; in the end I have known no knowledge I have been almost torn asunder in ignorance, degraded and abused and exhausted of myself but could not excape from my pursuer, lost in the most strangest love in all the world, the haunted love of myself. Oh I know that nowadays anybody wants to can have something taken away from their bodies or can have something added onto their bodies, can have more or can have less of something on their bodies so long as they've got a course of blood and a heart that pushes it through their veins, hear tell of, in cities—and once a man slipped a card to me in the Show that said he was such a doctor of repairs—of those that have new bosoms and new noses, all doctor-made. But not Arcadio, not Arcadio, not him. God told me to bring my separate parts to peace, *reconciliación* was the word, *Jesucristo* said I am a man of *reconciliación, un hombre de reconciliación,* that's why he was knocking on the door in the nighttime with the lantern in his hand. Oh many times when I have been afighting with myself and in a terrible fighting I have heard a knocking on my door. And so I begun to live in a truce between my tormented parts close together day and night, understand, closest of neighbors, else I'd have long ago been pulled apart, torn in two, a crazy man, or self-destroyed. Which I almost was, as you have heard me tell a little bit of. For that long time my spirit was damned because of my body. Isn't it surprising that what you have on your body can cause such tumult in your soul? Yet it twas my body got me to my soul, to *Jesucristo. Señor* that is aknocking, I cried out, how can I live with *este cuerpo* this body that you gave to me? It tears apart my soul. Well then give me your body, *Jesucristo* said. And so he reconciled. This is what happened to me, *Señor, Señora, Señorita.* I know all this that I tell you. If you wan hear. The Holy Spirit that I told you about has reconciled me whole and I am peaceful. So do you see that *Jesucristo* gave up his *cuerpo* for me, that his flesh was nailed to wood, that on the wood his flesh died forever, do you see what I'm saying, *comprendes?* And now knocks when there is trouble beyond the door where you and I sit weeping *llorando* or drinking *bebiendo* gin, dying *muriendo* alone, or in trouble with somebody, fighting at them and screaming in the terrible dance of death with them. And you will hear the knocking if you hold quiet and listen you will hear the soft knocking. And had I not found the White Bible, had that hand not handed it down to me, I would be dead I would be nailed dead by my own *cuerpo*, my own body, my own flesh, and had not my mother come, sent by *Jesucristo* to set me free from the Show where there was no real revealing. I will not look no longer for it. I could have been a dog beneath my clothes. People looked at an appearance, something that *looked like* something. There was no revelation. I would be in bondage, *Señor*, had I not excaped, and run from the Show under my *madre*'s auspices, *mi madre* before who I revealed myself at last, had I not turned over my body *mi cuerpo*—a very precious thing, *Señor*, to turn over to anybody—to the Holy Spirit. It would have damned me to the hell of feeling nailed to death on that wood, I know what I am talking about, you wan hear, I have come up living from those nails, the woman part has closed up like a flower closes and the man has given up its bitter sting on me. They are *espléndido*, at splendid rest. Reconciled, that is the word. I'm handiwork of God, I will be chaste, I will be a saint, I have been too much for myself and for the world, I will surrender my body to God, I'm handiwork of God, I'm looking for God, I'm on my way to God, I don miss the Show no more, I won't go back. You wan hear, you wan hear.

Sister and brother, wife and husband, lover and sweetheart, I have sometimes helped out in the world. In a town, for instance, that was hit by a tornado, I come upon a woman in a ditch, hurting in childbirth and the child would not come because of the woman's being so afraid and while a boy held up a coat in front of the hot blinding sun I caused with the softest softness a squalling baby to slip forth easy from the woman that had let go and opened. Doctor! the woman called out, husband, father, lover! And once when I come among men working on a railroad where one of them had fallen senseless in the heat, I kneeled over the man and put hands on his body and in this tenderness brought him to his senses. The men were drawn to me and the revived man touched my hair in softness. Mother, sister, wife, sweetheart, the man whispered. In a Sex Arcade in a city, I was the mop-man and I was clean-up man in Baths for a while and once in a brothel I was a nurse and companion to the women and I was clean with them, men and women, and I was pure to myself. You have heard how in the other days I was drunk and damned with feeling and wanting. How night and day in the dark whorehouse of Shuang Boy over the dead river that was like a dead soup, with planks and turds and condoms lying stagnant in it, how in that darkness of the *China Boy* I laid, you wan hear, with the hot mouths eating my body to death, my breasts was frosted with semen my eyes glued with that glue my stomach was spread with it like a mayonnaise, my hair set in a marcel of come and my face a running icing that strung down to my neck in pearl drops and there was a necklace of gold around my neck and the pieces of men and women like soggy peaches broken open sopping against me and hot tongues licked over every piece of me and there didn't seem no way out for me I was goin under I was dyin and I was in my hot death, *muerto, muerto, muriendo.* And once in the mirror in the dawn light I saw my ash-white face with the bitter smile of the *maldito* damned-in-the-flesh on it, the *demonio* of the fucked dying was on it, *perdido, perdido,* and over the dead river seen a little moon of salt. And *Jesucristo* was with me in all those places, *Oyente,* in the Baths and in the whore-house, too, you wan hear, and in the room of dying over the dead river, waiting for me to cry to him, softly knock-ing. And if you are sick of flesh and body and feeling and wanting and cannot put out of your mind pictures of the flesh, if you are haunted and in that bondage then you can remember me, you can recall my story and cry for the knocking *hombre de reconciliación,* or put it all aside as something that does not have nothing to do with you and *perdóname, Señor, Señora, Señorita, compadre, Corazón.* You wan hear?

Song of Tomasso

I HUNTED THEN Tomasso. When you are hunting somebody you think you see them everywhere but in this time I did not know what the object of my hunting looked like, *comprendes,* though I had a face of him before my eyes in my imagination.

Seen, at a place on a lake, one young man moving alone in a little boat on a gray lake on a gray day, twas up in Rhode Island, I had come up there, up that far, up to a completely lonely lake, outside Providence. Suddenly I asked myself could this rower be Tomasso my half brother? A Mescan Jew in Rhode Island? But I guess twas not my half brother Tomasso, whose mother was my mother. I went on.

Saw in a choir in the Deliverance Church in Norfork Virginia a handsome boy, paler than the others, white in his brownness, singing among the black people. Something strange about him. The pale choir singer haunted me, the movement of his body as he sang the way he joyfully clapped his hands not clapping them but holding them back from each other just a little before they come together and his hands spread wide open; he haunted me, this pale boy the way he flickered his eyes, flickering his brow with the joyful smile. Was he a Mescan boy living among the blacks, living and singing among the blacks? Something of Chupa in him. But guessed twas not my half brother Tomasso. But was this Tomasso, my half brother, whose mother was my mother? Could this be Tomasso, a Mescan Jew in a black choir?

I waited till the singing was done and when the singing was done I saw the dark eyes of the light-colored boy stare upon me drawing me and pulling me and *tenía miedo* I felt ascared but I could not turn away; and then I saw the light-colored boy come towards me.

When he was close upon me I seen the dark eyes and I seen something of *mi madre* on him, on his brow or over his face somewhere over his facial features I don know what and I seen my lips upon him those lips was mine come upon his mouth from me through our mother you know what I mean lips handed down sounds funny to hand down lips but tis Anglo tis not Mescan we have no such Mescan espression. Tomasso! I softly called and he said *Quién me llamas?* who calls? Tomasso! I cried and the light-colored boy said *Sí?* I am your brother, I said. *Sí* he said, all men are brothers, that is what the Deliverance Choir sings about, my brother. Where have you come from as a birthplace I asked him; and how come you say Mescan words? From a Missoura jail, he said and I said there is no doubt you are my brother—half—adding to that that you know Mescan, too, how come you know Mescan words. I have not told you our mother is the same woman, and that is why, of course; yet you never knew our mother, how can that be? From Hondo in the Missoura jail, Tomasso told me, taught me some Mescan words because he saw the brownness in me and guessed that I had some Mescan, which he is familiar with because he was borned in Arroyo Hondo in New Mexico. My mother run away from me and left me with Mr. and Mrs. Sam Policheck, the Bohunk jailer and his wife in a Missoura town. What is the name of it? I said, and Tomasso said I do not know the name of the town. I was only in jail in it and when I excaped I slid through a hole into the night and run. Thank God and *Jesucristo*, I said. When I found that my mother had run away, the light-colored boy said, I run away too. Wouldn't you? *Sí*, I said. Yes, very much. What is a Bohunk? I asked, and he said he did not know but that Hondo said that about Mr. Sam Policheck. And who is Hondo? I asked him and he said my wonderful friend that I will soon tell you about. But come with me, I said, for I have news of your mother. Who I never saw, said Tomasso. Nor my father neither, added Tomasso. Him I have no direct news of, I said. But your mother, yes. Except to say that your father is dead, killed by the police long ago. Tomasso cried. *Perdóname* for such sad *noticias*, I said, but this is according to our mother Chupa's story. Chupa? Tomasso asked me. Her name, the name of your mother. Tomasso cried. How many times have I imagined my mother, cried Tomasso. She is beautiful, I told him. How old are you? Twelve, he said. Well, your mother is *una loca*, you cannot count on her. But she has *la anima* which means life; and has *el amor* which means love and tries to give them out to somebody but has brought her many troubles. And so she runs. I can tell this to you but I cannot too much understand it myself. It is strange how we can do this, tell somebody else what we cannot understand ourselves, *verdad? Verdad*, answered Tomasso. You know that word, too, I said. *Sí,* said Tomasso, from Hondo; but what is your name, you have not told me. Arcadio, I told him. It is a beautiful name, said Tomasso; as beautiful almost as Hondo. Anyway, I said, I have been looking for our mother and for you. Now you will come with me to look for her. Together we will find her and she will be glad to find us both—for a little while, I guess.

Tomasso come away from Deliverance Church with me that night leaving Deliverance Choir one hundred *por ciento* black. He was so glad to have him a half blood brother, he had been very lonesome though the black people were very kind to him and his only family until I come. Arcadio! Arcadio! he cried and embraced me and laid his head on my shoulder. Arcadio! my half brother! Tomasso! Tomasso! I cried, holding him, my little half blood brother, my jailboy, choirboy I love you!

We went on together. I read him from the White Bible and told him the stories, I nursed and watched after him the jailboy Tomasso, my mother's son, I was mother and father to him. God, after waiting awhile, brought the jailboy's parents to him in me, the *Biblia* showed me this, says *mine own will come to me, La Biblia Blanca* showed me about life, *La Biblia* give me words and give me understanding. I run in the jailyard, Tomasso said. I played with the convicts, the trusties. What's the trusties, I said, Tomassito? The ones you could trust, said he, my friends Hondo and Old John. They helped me to excape, they cried as they helped me, to see me go. I crawled under a fence through a hole they dug by a Rose a Sharon. What is a Rose a Sharon? I says. A beautiful tree of blooms, answered Tomasso. I run all night panting and ascared. As if I was a convict! And I run all day, day after day. Until I got to Deliverance Church and they took me in. Here is a curl of black hair Hondo give me to keep, tis from the head of Sweet Janine. This is what Tomasso told me, you wan hear. Said Hondo killed his sweetheart Sweet Janine of sixteen because he did not know his own strength. We do not know our own strength, I said. *Sí* said Tomasso, this is what Hondo the trusty taught me that we do not know our own strength. How could he know that he was choking Sweet Janine to death, Hondo said, that night when he was so full of loving for her? She was *una virgen* and went to Virgin's Heaven, Tomasso related to me. Are you a *virgen* he asked me and I said what? and he said this is a virgin's hair off the head of a virgin killed by a man who did not know his own strength, Hondo; he give it to me to hold for good luck until he can excape and find me. Which will be when he and Old John can make the hole larger. Every night they are adigging. Uh-huh, I says. Virgin's Heaven, Tomasso continued to tell me, was a place of small population for you had to be sixteen to make it. I would not have made it at ten, I said to myself, and I wondered what Tomasso would have thought of my wild boyhood in the *China Boy*. If I had told him he'd have run away I am sure. My pure sweet brother, my saint brother, I cried to Tomasso, I will not let nothing hurt you I will be your mother and father. I loved Tomasso more than anything ever in this world, you wan hear. I sat under a tree while he climbed up in it and I heard him singing up there in his boy's voice, clear like a sweet bird and oh will he fly away from me, I wondered, like his mother will he fly away? I bathed him in clean creeks and washed his long black hair, black, black and saw his brown body turning in the silver water and wondered would he ride on down the current of the creek and down the falls under the tunnel of the low trees and ride away from me in the dark tunnel of the trees. Once he cut his foot and I carried him all day upon my hip he rode there like a warm brown animal and at nights he folded upon my breast. When some boys came upon Tomasso in a street I moved into them like a lion, *feroz*, and scattered them away. I threw one up into a tree, we run on hearing the cries from the tree. I did not know my own strength, like Hondo. Nobody was going to hurt Tomasso, nobody was going to harm the hair of his head nor cause one bit of pain to him. Wonder will he die, I thought, my God will he get sick? I thought my God love is too much for me to do, the feelings that love brings me washes me over like a wave I feel like I am drownding why did I ever hunt and find my brother, is this what brother's love is, pain and ascared to lose them? And sometimes I felt my mother's nature in me that I wanted you wan hear to run away, I wanted to excape. This made me feel so bad that I run and grabbed him up and held him full of fear and pain against my breast until he cried agasping Arcadio Arcadio what is there trying to get us what is after us why are you afraid and shaking and tears are falling on me from your eyes, Arcadio don't be afraid God and *Jesucristo* will protect us like you say like *La Biblia Blanca* says that you read out to me, *Lo I am always with you even to the end of the world.* Remember Arcadio? he says. And I says out to him with all my tears, *sí recuerdo*, I remember, do not be afraid, *no tienes miedo.* Tell me that you'll never leave me like your mother did. You wan hear.

It was very hard for me to find one thing of my mother's ways in him. Except maybe for his staying to himself, for his *solitario* part. Otherwise he was as gentle as the little white jumping dog which once I loved so much and that loved me. Yet sometimes I would catch a look across his face that was my mother's, a look of *mi madre* would brush across, something *misterioso;* but Tomasso's lips upon his mouth was mine. God knows what features his Jewish father showed up on him, this we would never be able to tell until we found our mother who would recognize the marks that could be left on somebody by a one day's loving.

Together we went on, my half brother Tomasso and me, hunting for our mother. Will we soon see Chupa our mother? Tomasso would ask. I don know I says. Will Chupa *mi madre* maybe be in this town? Tomasso would ask. *Quizás,* I said. We'll look. Is she very beautiful? asked Tomasso. *Sí,* I says. And every night Tomasso would say in his prayers God help me and my brother Arcadio to find our mother Chupa soon. And oh I wanted to bring this son and this mother, this boy and this woman together and that was what I prayed in my prayer to God and *Jesucristo,* hep me do hep me bring this boy to his mother and show this mother this boy that she carried under a green fringe dress until she broke him out of her and left him in the Missoura jail as soon as she could walk and before his eyes could see. And we hunted and we hunted asingin and aprayin as we went.

One time in a town we followed a woman and watched her all day where she went, twas a dark flashing woman that could be Chupa, all day we watched and followed her, oh she went here and she went there and we followed her and finally when she was on a phone aphoning we stood close to her but what she was aphoning was *la policía* upon us and when they come and tried to apprehend us, all we told them was that we thought this woman was our mother and that we had long lost her and not to please apprehend us and those *policía* said you two sons of a lost mother that you are hunting are not going to be taken in and apprehended into a jail but are going to be given an outstanding award of twenty-two dollars and fifty *centavos* because this woman is Lou Jones a crooked woman that we have long hunted for in three counties of this state, thank you very much. What is a crooked woman, Tomasso asked me and I said I don know we have no such espression. And we rejoiced me and Tomasso and you may ask *Oyente* what we done with the twenty-two dollars and fifty cents reward, give a tithe of it like the White Bible told me to, give two dollars of it to a mission of the town for the pore, then bought two warm blankets in a J. C. Penney's with some more of the twenty-two fifty and then bought us a whole bunch of *tamales* and ate some and kept some for the days ahead. But the woman, you wan hear, was not Chupa.

Since his singing was so beautiful he sung in railroad stations or we would stand on corners in some cities or by fountains in the nighttime and sing our songs; and sometimes in a park, alone, singing and playing at twilight to the air and to ourselves; twas so peaceful, twas so beautiful; and I taught Tomasso many songs, some of them very beautiful that I had heard the Mescans sing, in my boyhood, one called "*Lágrimas,*" tears. *Lágrimas de dolor, lágrimas dolorosas, negro es el color de nuestras tristezas,* and some gay ones that the women sung in the *China Boy, I don't care, I don't care;* and some songs from the Show that the Dwarft Eddy sung, were little soft songs, not like the tough Dwarft that he was to us, songs about that the old gray goose is dead and of the wind of the western sea—*blow, blow, come and go, wind of the west-*

ern sea—nothing you would expect from a pessimistic Dwarft; but no songs from Old Shanks he never sung a fucking word, please excuse the language but I still get mad when his old name is mentioned, even if it's me amentioning it; and many songs from Tomasso's days of the Deliverance Choir, such as "Lullaby of Jesus, Baby," "Sweeten the Bitter Waters," and oh the sad one

> I'll see you again one day, baby,
> O'er the crystal strand. Baby.
> When we will meet again. Baby.
> Do not cry for me.

What is a crystal strand, I says to Tomasso. I do not know, says Tomasso. It's what we sung. And of course my special number as a solo was "The Waltz of the Spotted Dog," my old Show tune and the only one I knew, goes like this:

don you like it. But oh when Tomasso sung it with some words that he made up, my heart cried for the sweetness of his song not to mention my eyes that would drop salted tears into my rusty frenchharp as I played for him—cain't remember the words you'd have to ask him but you cain't he's gone. Tomasso's song! Asinging! People loved his singing and they give us money for it, his voice was sweet to hear, wish you could've heard it wish that I could hear it now, asinging here, wish could sing it for you but I cain't. We was cold and we was hungry. But the child sung. Poor and ascared sometimes and hungry and without a home, but the child sung. How can I explain to you why the child sings? I says. How can I myself understand why a child such as this would sing? Without a home and hungry and huntin for his mother? What is singing, anyway, what is a song? You wan hear. I loved so much my half blood brother Tomasso and I was happy with him. What if this wasn't the real Tomasso you would say to me and I would answer that since I had never known him anyway and did not know what to espect, this one, Tomasso or not, would do. Tomasso or not. You wan hear. Probably just as good as Tomasso if not better because how did I know what Tomasso's faults would have been if this was not the real Tomasso you wan hear. I might have hated him. And this way I could find many Tomassos of my *own*, many brothers. And anyway *La Biblia Blanca* says that we are all brothers. You wan hear? And there would be many a man wandering hunting for a brother. So Tomasso and I was happy. And would be so happy the day we would come across our mother Chupa. And whether Chupa would be happy would be another story (which may never be told, I do not know). What a day twould be, you wan hear, *compadre*. And so until then there was Tomasso singing, out of nothing, but singing his song out of the life, *la vida*, joyfully singing at my side, out of the hungriness, *el hambre*, why was he so glad? out of no home, out of no mother nor father, singing joyful at the side of an old half brother; Tomasso sang. If I could sing his song for you! If I could put back breath in his dead song! But it is gone now, singing only in my memory. And you will never hear it, you wan hear.

And you wan hear, *compadre*, that that day that we would find our mother Chupa never come oh tis sorrowful to tell. Oh is it all sorrow that I have to sing? All losing and ahunting? No because you will remember that you've heard the joy part of my song, remember? How much joy part would there be in yours, *Señor, Señorita,* if you was to sing your song to me? You wan hear. Yet for a little while we went asinging on and huntin. But we kept our eye out for posses just like I had during the days of my own excape, as I have told you about. If somebody had tried to capture my brother I would have killed them. And sometimes we was sure that certain people was trying to capture Tomasso. When they would ask what school you go to, *niño* little boy, then we would go away before they could espect an answer. Then we would hide in cotton gins if twas wintertime and if we was down in the cotton country. And once in a cotton town Tomasso cried out Hondo! and run away into a crowd and I could not find Tomasso and was scared that he had run away to Hondo that had finally made the hole big enough and had excaped; but in a little while Tomasso come on back to me sad and said it twas not Hondo. Then I was ascared for some days because I knew that Tomasso was alooking for his Hondo and hopin that he would excape and come and find him with the curl of hair. But then the scaredness passed away and back come our sweet days, seem like now that they did not ever happen just perfect days of sweetness maybe was a dream I do not know sometimes now as I sing my song of days of yore.

11

Hondo's Song

B UT ONE DAY THERE was Hondo standing on a corner in a town of a green bayou. I heard a cry Hondo! and twas Tomasso running to a big gray man. Tomasso! the man called back. I dug the hole finally big enough! Hondo Hondo! cried Tomasso. Where is the curl of Sweet Janine's hair? asked Hondo. And when Tomasso pulled out the Bull Durham sack and pulled out the curl of little hair, the gray man seized up Tomasso and whirled him in the air, twas a joyful reunion. I was ahunting you, said Hondo, at the same time as I am going on my way to find Sweet Janine's sister Ethelreda Johansson, they are Swedish people. Bohunks? I asked. No, said Hondo, the Missoura jailer Sam Policheck is a Bohunk. I told him said Tomasso. Hondo, this is Arcadio my half blood brother. I am Hondo Holloway, Hondo Holloway says and shook my hand and I fell down alittle from his crushing squeeze and said my God what strength. I am on my way to make amends to Sweet Janine's big sister, said Hondo to me. Because you did not know your own strength I says to Hondo Holloway. I told him, says Tomasso. Tis a terrible thing when somebody does not know their own strength, I says. Then Tomasso asked Hondo where was Old John. Sick in the Missoura jail he may now be dead, Hondo told Tomasso. Very tired from helping dig the hole for you and for me. Tomasso cried. Do not cry, said Hondo, God will bless Old John for helping you and me to excape, do not fear, said soft kind Hondo Holloway.

I guess I never met a sweeter man than Hondo. It was one of the presents that Tomasso give to me. Got his name from the *arroyo* he said was borned near Arroyo Hondo in New Mexico, grew up with the Mescans of Nuevo Méjico but was of *gringo* parents name of Holloway. Hondo had a sweet face of hair, face covered with a soft gray beard and two gray eyes asparkling out, Hondo was a gray soft furry man. And of a deep low voice that you would not think would ever raise up against anybody yet he killed Sweet Janine with's love. Because he did not know his own strength. Hondo said he was hunting for Sweet Janine's sister Ethelreda Johansson so that he could present to her the curl of little hair and beg her to forgive him for the accidental death of Sweet Janine, accidental even though he was thrown into the Missoura jail to stay for his lifetime for murder of Sweet Janine— the word that Hondo told me that they used: *homicidio.* Hondo took out an almost rubbed-out picture of two women, one a beautiful girl of streaming hair and the other a great big woman with a big head and arms, and *grande.* The big *grande* woman will not forgive you Hondo, I said. It's just not in her I told him you can see in the picture that it's just not in her. Well I have to try, said Hondo. I spent some time digging with Old John— my strength was weak—a hole big enough to excape out of the Missoura jail so that I could ask the forgiveness of

Sweet Janine's sister, and Old John give his life, looks like it's going to be, for it. I cannot rest until I do, I will not have no peace, no inner peace until I come before Janine Johansson's sister Ethelreda. Which is a hard name for a Mescan to say, Ethelreda, you wan hear.

Why don't we all go together since we are all ahunting for people, I says, Tomasso and me for our *madre* Chupa and me for my father Hombre and sometimes for the Show, you for your dead sweetheart's sister. But are we all going in the same direction? asked Hondo. I have been traveling northwest. In what part of the country did you murder Sweet Janine, I asked. Please do not use that word Hondo begged me, but I do not remember since I was blacked-out in my wild strength of loving Sweet Janine and I run out of whatever state it was in such blindness after I saw what I had done. But, said Hondo, I have long had a hunch through many many dreams of Sweet Janine that her sister could be found in the Northwest somewhere. How did the posse catch you I asked Hondo, for you were at large as I was and had a posse—ridiculous as it was, composed of Shanks and a mean little Dwarft—I had a posse huntin for me, too; how did they get you? That is another story Hondo said. I had such visions in my dreams or even suddenly when I was awake of Sweet Janine. She was in a field of bluebonnets all in a white dress ablowing. But you should be going toward the Southwest, said I to Hondo Holloway, for there is where the bluebonnets bloom. In Texas, my home. But I have dreamt of Sweet Janine's sister Ethelreda standing in the Northwest. What did you see about the Northwest in your dream, I asked. Maybe I can help you I have been in almost every town since I have been at large. I don want talk about it right now, says Hondo and when he patted me on the back I went over to one side from the blow even though he was apatting me, because he did not know his own strength. Maybe you should see a Medium, *Una Médium*, I suggested to Hondo, a Medium could show you about the *visiones* that you had of Sweet Janine and could help you get a message. Twas *Una Médium* in the Show that people paid a dollar to, to get a message from *los muertos* the dead ones. Was she a gypsy, said Hondo. I don know, said: she was under twenty-seven veils and her name was Orisana. At's a gypsy, says Hondo, sounds like to me. Well under the twenty-seven veils, I don know, I says. But I do know that one night man from a town come after her with a shotgun because said got a message from his first wife when Orisana promised message from his second. Shanks had to put Orisana behind locked doors where she cried out how could I help it it's not my problem that he kept marrying women named Louise, wrong one answered, how the fuck could I help it if everybody's named Louise? Where is Orisana, Hondo asked me. Know where can I find this Medium? I would pay her anything. I have saved up quite a bundle from the little Savings and Loan. What is a bundle? I asked. Well quite a whole lot, Hondo said. From the little Savings and Loan Bank in some town, I can't remember. Maybe it was in Janine's town, I says, where you accidentally murdered her. Please not to use that word, asked Hondo. You took some money from the little bank, you robbed the little Savings and Loan? I asked Hondo. Something similar to that, answered Hondo. But that is a sin and you will have to return the money, I told Hondo. I will never be able to do that, said Hondo, because I buried most of it in the ground under the Missoura jail, in a baitbox. You was always adiggin in the Missoura jail I says to Hondo. But

ARCADIO

79

now you'll have to leave the buried money to God. God and *Jesucristo*'ll have to dig for it. And Old John, added Hondo, who is a very rich man. And locked up in a jail, and dying, I says, and cain't dig anymore. Is that rich? I says. But if you would like, I would go as a servant of God and *Jesucristo* to the Missoura jail and by night help you dig up the Savings and Loan so that you could return it to where you sinfully took it if you could remember the town. Then you would be forgiven and freed from the Missoura jail, confessing to the jailer Policheck. No, Hondo told me, that would do no good, although I appreciate the offer, because I was not in jail for the Savings and Loan but because of the accidental death of Sweet Janine. Oh my God I am all mixed up, I says. I am not able to figure out about the Savings and Loan. Was it before the death of Sweet Janine or after? How could it be after since I was grabbed at once by the police and thrown into jail, says Hondo. Where was all the Savings and Loan, I asked when the police grabbed you. Hidden all over me, explained Hondo. It was Old John that had the baitbox to put it in. Where was Old John, I asked. Already in the jail. I'm all mixed up, I says, Hondo. So am I, says Hondo. Anyways, he says, I brought quite a bit of the Savings and Loan through the hole of excape. So where is the Medium that can get a message from Sweet Janine? I will pay her anything. Escuse my asking, Hondo, I says, but where is the Savings and Loan? Hidden, says Hondo. Hidden safely against my groins. Not safely, I says. That is the first place *La Médium* goes. What for? asked Hondo. To help you to get the message I says. So where is she? asked Hondo again. Orisana? I says. *La Médium?* I don know, I says, where to find the Show. If you would help me hunt for the Show then we could find Orisana—

quizás perhaps she may still be with the Show I don know. Some days I think I will come back to it but then I do not even know where is the old Show. You need a Medium too, said Tomasso. To get a message where the Show is. But the Medium and the Show are in the same place—if they are anywhere in this world any longer, I said. And we don even know where that is says Hondo, listen we are huntin for too much I'm all mixed up. I thought we were looking for my mother, said pore little Tomasso. Well I will help you hunt for the Show, Arcadio, says Hondo, and that of course includes the Medium, but only if the Show is in the same direction as Ethelreda Johannson, which is northwest. O.K. I says, who knows but what the Show is not in that direction. And the Medium, added Tomasso. And since we don know which direction to go anyway, because we don know where anybody is that we are ahuntin . . . let's go northwest, says Hondo.

So that is how we all went off together in the same direction, Tomasso and Hondo Holloway and me. I was sure there was a posse out ahuntin for Hondo so we kept out an eye. *Jesucristo* always something to keep out an eye for, either for somethin you're ahuntin or for something huntin you, my God what is this life what is this world? You wan hear? But somewhere on the way, in some town, Hondo pointed to a sign that read GLORIA OX MEDIUM GET A MESSAGE FROM THOSE GONE BEFORE YOU. That would be Sweet Janine I says to Hondo, gone before you. And with some help from you, I says to myself but not so's Hondo could hear. If you could speak to Sweet Janine through Gloria Ox the Medium then you would no longer have to hunt for her sister but could make amends direct to Sweet Janine, I told Hondo. Or through Gloria Ox, said Hondo. Already I see that you have your mind quite a bit on the Medium more than the message, I said to Hondo. I am somewhat acquainted with these Mediums because of esperiences in the past, I was remembering of course Orisana in the Show, under twenty-seven veils. Sometimes they look so pretty with the veils that a customer would seek the message of the Medium and forget, until later, what was the real message that he had come for—of those gone before you, *los muertos.* Until afterwards when *La Médium* had satisfied the customer's lonesomeness and vanished. You mean fucked the customer instead of putting the customer in touch with *los muertos* the deceased? asked Hondo. *Sí*, I says. And rolled him. I am very lonely and have not put it into a woman for some time, Hondo told me. Well I hope the Medium Gloria Ox is not going to look too pretty, you might get the messages mixed up, I said. Well, if the Medium was pretty I would have to think twice, said Hondo to me, because I badly need both messages. Well pay some attention to the veils, the veils can hide an old trout, I says to Hondo. My God and *Jesucristo* you should have seen what was revealed when Orisana lifted some of her twenty-seven veils. What was it? asked Hondo. An old trout—*una trucha vieja.* Well, answered Hondo, in my condition an old trout don't sound too bad. If that's what you want, I told him. An old trout.

Well, Hondo was so *loco* for *noticias* of Sweet Janine—and for some lifting of the veils, too, that he right away showed his Savings and Loan to Gloria Ox or what I believe is that Gloria Ox right away detected it hidden in his groins and Gloria Ox told Hondo that to get the message he would have to leave us and stay alone with her for seven days then maybe seven more; and so we said *adiós*

to Hondo and Tomasso cried to lose his old jail friend
and how he would miss touching the curl of little hair but
I esplained the best I could; but pore little Tomasso cried
that he could not *comprende* the ways of men about a
woman and I said *cállate muñeco* quieten yourself little
doll one day you will. Never mind, I said, as on we wan-
dered, we will meet up again with Hondo Holloway when
God and *Jesucristo*—and Gloria Ox—wants to bring us
back together again; but that day never come which is
what I soon will have to sing you, oh is it all sorrow that I
have to sing? All losing and ahunting? No because you
will remember that you've heard the joy part of my song,
remember? How much joy part would there be in your
song, *Señor, Señorita, Oyente,* if you was to sing your
song to me? You wan hear.

But oh my God and *Jesucristo* my brother was not
ever going to see his old jail friend again my brother was
not long for me to keep as I will now begin to sing to you.
You wan hear? For on one night of darkest darkness, not
one moon above, I woke up and I felt a cold against me
and twas Tomasso cold against me, 'gainst my breast, and
did not speak and did not move. And then I run in the
night with Tomasso cold to a hospital of a town had a red
cross and when they took him from my arms they said
who are you who is this child and took him from me. O
Oyente I fell down on my knees and begged do not take
Tomasso from me and cried to God and *Jesucristo* where
are you? and O *Oyente* I am cryin now to still remember
it do not take away Tomasso oh God heal him *Jesucristo*
reach to him Tomasso touch him like you touched all
those others that I read in the White Bible *los ciegos y los
sordos y los cojos* the blind boy and the deaf boy and the
lame and the even dead man that you brought up again,

restore Tomasso! But the people took Tomasso and they would not let me in I do not know why. I slept on the doorstep all that night awaiting for the morning and for the people to come give me back Tomasso. And then they come and said who are you do you have any identification and I said I am this boy's half brother our mother was the same her name is Chupa and we have been huntin for her. Where did you find the boy they said and I said at Deliverance Church asingin. What is wrong with him I asked and they said he is dead, *muerto muerto*; and I cried oh my God what from, dead? From a disease the people said and I said what was his disease. And they said hunger. *Hunger* they said: O do not cry *Oyente* oh I hear you cry. I did not know, *Oyente*, that sweet Tomasso was so hungry that he died. I called out to the people he did not have the hunger he sung. But the people closed the door and would not give Tomasso back to me. And I laid all day back of a shed in the bushes and could not lift up my head and could not see I had fallen down blind and could not speak a word I had been struck down *mudo*.

When dark come I got up and knew what God and *Jesucristo* told me to do. I crawled to a window and saw through it under a light the pale brown body of Tomasso fair and beautiful in his blessed brownness that our mother give to him and I cried oh you Chupa *madre madre* where are you now? I stole with the help of God and *Jesucristo* the boy Tomasso's body from the place they had him and run all through the night aholdin him against my breast, aspeakin over and over to cold Tomasso but you was not hungry *no tenías hambre* you was not hungry tell me that you was not hungry. Cause I fed you and I watched you eat and I heard you sing you *sung*; run all night aholding to my breast the pure *Jesucristo cuerpo* body of Jesus Tomasso the pure body that *Jesucristo* lived in I am sure. Maybe it was *Jesucristo* himself come and walked awhile with me, all through Kansas Alabama and Wyoming and then departed from my sight. Maybe twas *Jesucristo* looking like a Mescan-Jewish boy of twelve. Because one time you know that a stranger walked along the road with the two disciples and talked with them and even sat and ate with them and they thought something was different about the stranger and then it dawned on them it was the very Lord Jesus *Jesucristo!* And oh they was so full of joy because they had been blue since *Jesucristo* had been gone. Tis in the *Biblia Blanca* you will find it there. Run all night to Deliverance Church in Norfork Virginia to the Reverence Carl C. Cane and delivered dead Tomasso to Deliverance Choir where first I found him singin and aclappin his brown hands. Oh God and *Jesucristo!* And oh that Choir sung, sung for the dead boy Tomasso come back home and oh they clapped their hands and wailed out and they wept like Jesuses friends wept at the foot of the cross and Deliverance Choir delivered sweet Tomasso up to Virgin's Heaven.

Deliverance Choir wanted me to stay and Reverence C. Carl Cane—just say C.C. says the Reverence, like many people do, then they don't have the problem of which comes first the C. or the Carl. Thank you C.C. I says. I only wish I had known this earlier. Anyways the Reverence C.C. Cane wanted me to stay at Deliverance Church in Norfork Virginia with all of the wonderful Choir and all of the wonderful Choir wanted me to, too. Can Deliverance Choir use a frenchharp I asked them? We could sure find a place for a mouth organ says Reverence C.C. Cane. I have never heard it called that, I says.

My grandfather played one, says Reverence C.C. Cane. In the Blue Ridge. Twas strapped around his mouth while he played a fiddle. How would that work? I says. Wouldn't the sawing of his arm knock the frenchharp out of's mouth? This sometimes happened, says the Reverence.

But I went on, waving goodbye to all the wonderful Deliverance Choir of Tomasso that was asinging *I'll see you again one day, baby, O'er the crystal strand. Baby. When we will meet again. Baby. Do not cry for me.* I had delivered Tomasso back to Deliverance Choir and Deliverance Choir had delivered him into Virgin's Heaven. As far as I could go that night I heard their heavenly singin blowing over and around me on the wind, oh twas so sad.

And I wished again that I had never found Tomasso, never come upon him in Deliverance Choir, wished I'd never found him, he might still be live and singin with his blessed family of black brothers and sisters in Deliverance Church under the leadership of Carl C. Cane or was it C. Carl Cane cain't now remember exactly, C. C., that's right, C. C., aclappin his brown hands the way he did, asmilin, my jailboy, my *virgen* singer, my sweet brother, my mother Chupa's own son with a Jewish salesman.

I remember now what he said that when the person told him that he had a mother somewhere said that he run to Mr. and Mrs. Policheck the Bohunks, and asked them. But said that Mr. and Mrs. Sam Policheck would never tell him one thing about his mother and mine. Said he said why is it such a dark secret and said they said it is so dark that even we do not even know anything. Your mother was mum about herself, had sealed her own lips, they said (these are Anglo espressions we do not have any Mescan for them, to seal lips and to keep mum) so said he sealed his own lips too, Tomasso did and never again after he was seven years of age asked about his mother but vowed to one day excape and look for *noticias* of her in the world. So one night with the help of Hondo and Old John through the hole they dug, he run out into the night and was soon found by the Reverence . . . Carl . . . C. . . . Cane and was taken—I *think* the Carl comes first—he was twelve and joyous—into Deliverance Church. Instead of finding my mother, Tomasso said, in his Missoura accent, cain't say the way he said it in Missourian no matter what I say sounds Mescan Texas or out of *La Biblia* from learning to read by it and always reading from it and having its words; instead of finding my mother, Tomasso said, I found Deliverance Church and wonderful Brother C. Carl Cane. He convinced me to give up looking for my mother and to surrender her to Jesus, and to give myself to Deliverance Choir.

First about my life as a jailboy, Tomasso said, twas like a convict life. Mr. and Mrs Policheck seemed to forget that I was not a convict. They seemed to forget the same about each other, for they let each other in and out of the Missoura jail cells with big keys. They had, as Reverence C. Carl Cane said, a prison mentality, Tomasso said. Said Mrs. Nan Policheck was his teacher and school was the jail cell and that when he was astudyin he often would look up through the little jail window and wish he could excape; and then the little window was filled up with Instant Cement so that he would not have daydreams of excaping and would study, Tomasso told me. But said Nan Policheck—that was her name, Nan—said Nan Policheck held a little Sunday School in the jail cell on Sundays and taught him *Biblia* lessons, said he wrote out on the wall sayings from *La Biblia, God Loves Me* and *Suffer the little children to come unto Me*, and said he asked Nan Policheck why did little children have to suffer and said Nan Policheck answered because they are little children and Tomasso said he thought to himself that don't make any sense I will ask Hondo later but when he later asked Hondo Hondo said he didn't know. Let's see where was I oh yes, somehow he said, Tomasso said, he felt he was apaying in the Missoura jail for the sins of his unknown mother. But she had committed the crime, not him, and he wondered many nights layin awake in his sad bed of an orphan and a prison what in the world his mother's crime could be. I says to myself I'll wait to tell him that she stole a green dress with sparkled fringe, that was her crime. And said that he ate meals at the long table with the convicts, Hondo and Old John, lousy jail grub, said. Who were the others? I asked, and Tomasso said no others, only Hondo and Old John, except for town drunks or burglars in for a few days but not to stay, somebody bought them, come with money, bailed them out was the espression. But nobody come with money for me, said Tomasso, and I used to pray that somebody, maybe my mother, would show up with some cash for me and bail me out. That is an espression I have never heard, I said. My mother did show up, showed up at the Show, I says, but not with money, I was not bailed out. I begun to get sick, Tomasso said, wonderin what I was in for, what my sentence was that I was imprisoned as a prisoner in a jail, why I could not go to school with other kids or go to town. What do you mean sentence I asked my brother and he said I cain't hardly esplain it to you. Well I says tis a *gringo* espression, we have no such Mescan espression. And Tomasso says sentence means like a fine or something, the number of time you have to

pay for the crime you done. We have no such Mescan espression I told him. But go on about the jail I'm getting
all mixed up with different things agoing in my mind, and
different words and espressions, my God; it was a sad little life for a *niño* boy like you, I said. I could begin to
have thoughts of blaming that *chalupa* Chupa our
mother and to think that once again she's gone and hurt
her sons, that she only give us hurt! God damn why did
she do that, God damn, forgive me God and *Jesucristo*
but here is another *ejemplo* example of that woman's
hurt that she caused others. That's why we got to find our
mother, so we can get over these feelings, especially so I
can, I told Tomasso; to settle these hurts. And then to
forgive her, said Tomasso. Reverence C. Carl Cane told
me to forgive my mother. Reverence Carl C. Cane is
right, I says, tis the very teachings of our Lord and Savior
Jesucristo as tis told us in the White Bible. C. Carl Cane,
said Tomasso. The C. is first. O.K. I says. Where is the
virgen's hair? Here in my pocket in the little Bull Durham sack Hondo give me, says Tomasso. Let me see it, I
says, and Tomasso took out the Bull Durham sack and
took out the little soft hair and I touched it. A virgin's,
Tomasso said. *Sí*, I said. *Una virgen.* He looked a look at
me that was agoing to ask me the question and I says
don't ask me that again, *muñeco.*

I wish now that I had found out what sweet Tomasso thought of me I wish now that I had asked him
more questions, I wish now that I had asked all my listeners more questions. Even in the Show I wish that I had
asked my gazers questions, we could have had some conversations, I wish that I had torn the lock on the door and
torn the bars from the windows and invited people from
the town to visit me in my jewel glass wagon. We could

have had a conversation. *Quizás* perhaps I would not now have to sing so much if I had had some conversations. Sometimes we do not know who we are talking to like the *Biblia Blanca* story of the stranger walking on the road. And it was *Jesucristo* come again! Sometimes I do not know if being found is being lost, if who I find is who I lose, I only wander, looking and singing, everthing is taken from me 'cept the love of *Jesucristo*, soon I will not hunt and search no more, I will set down somewhere in love of God and seeing *Jesucristo* at my side. If people that I find do not run away from me they sink away from me cold upon my breast. I'm always left alone again. At least I have been twice, *mi madre* and Tomasso. *Jesucristo* will not go, he will not go.

But in a town in the rain I saw in a shed a man looked like Hondo and I got under the shed and saw that twas Hondo Holloway. *Abrazo! Abrazo!* I cried—but don't hug me too hard you do not know your own strength—and we had a reunion. But oh you are ahuggin a sad individual, I says, since I lose you a terrible thing has happened, I am heartbroke, I said to Hondo. And I told Hondo the *desgracia* misfortune of the blessed little Tomasso. We cried and Hondo said oh my God, said what happened to my boy Tomasso. He was hungry I said acryin. Well didn't you give him something to eat? He ate! I cried. Tomasso ate! And yet the people said he died of hunger. *Hambre? Hambre?* I cried out crazy. Hondo help me; that he died of hunger? He never said that he was hungry! *Hunger!* I cried to Hondo. *Hunger!* Hondo said you goan go *loco* on that word. I don know any of the particulars of what happened but it would seem to me that God took Tomasso by starving him on earth, our food on earth did not feed him. So, I whispered to

Hondo, *Jesucristo* in *La Biblia Blanca* said that you can eat and eat of this bread but you will still be hungry. Hondo said I believe Tomasso was meant to go to Heaven. *Virgen's* Heaven, I says. *Sí*, answered Hondo. He has joined with Sweet Janine. They both was meant to go to Heaven. Not for this earth, I says, and was acryin. You cryin? said Hondo. I guess a little I says. You? I guess a little, Hondo says. The boy's worth some of our cryin, some tears, I says. And the sweet girl too, says Hondo, and we cried together for Tomasso that we had loved so much and had gone on. But I did not cry so much for Sweet Janine because I never did know her. My face is full of tears, I says. And here's a big tear fell on my hand, said Hondo. I have had me some esperience with the sweet ones that make the big tears fall so you can listen to me, Hondo consoled me. It's fuckin hard to lose the little sweet ones in this old world. I shed my tears over that and am workin to make amends of forgiveness. So am I Hondo, I says. And we cried some more a little and thanked God and *Jesucristo* that we was together again.

I will not now tell you of my adventure with the Medium Gloria Ox, Hondo said to me, we will save that one for a rainy day. But this is one, I says to Hondo, a rainy day. Tis an espression, says Hondo. O.K. I says, *Jesucristo* another *gringo* espression. I will wait to hear of your esperience with Gloria Ox. I will only add that it was a misfortune a *desgracia*, said Hondo Holloway, and that she put me in touch with not one message. I bet that Gloria Ox is now in touch with all your money I says, I bet that was the message, I says. And, said Hondo, tried to run away into the night with it while I was waiting in the dark room without any of my clothes on. I said will you let me ask you one more question Hondo and Hondo says you can ask it. Was Gloria Ox a pretty lady, once she took off all them veils? An old trout, said Hondo—and a dead trout now. Oh my God you didn't not know your own *fuerza* strength again, I told him. I was only trying to get my Savings and Loan back, said Hondo Holloway. Well now you are double at-large, I says. And for the second time a posse is after you, my God two posses. We are deep in trouble, what shall we do? Go in a northwest direction like we started before the two *desgracias* hit us, said Hondo. Towards Ethelreda Johansson. O.K., I says. While I am huntin for *mi madre* and sometimes the Show I will help you try and find Sweet Janine's sister Ethelreda, I told him. But now we'll have to keep out eyes for *three* posses, two posses for you and one posse (an old one) for me, *Jesucristo* always somethin to keep out an eye for, either for somethin you're ahuntin or for somethin ahuntin you, my God what is this life what is this world? Where is the little sack of Janine's hair did Gloria Ox get that? I have the little hair, said Hondo, and here it is. And you will never guess where it was hidden. Now I don wan sing much of this part but I will say that Hondo was the best friend ever that I had and the only friend when you get right down to it. You wan hear.

To not to know your own *fuerza* give Hondo Holloway some problems. *Por ejemplo* for example he was ascared of so much that he become the lonesomest man in the world. Why would anybody want to let him give them an *abrazo*, hug em? They might get all their backbones cracked. Why would anybody want that? I got to help you learn about your *fuerza* how much you can take ahold of anything or somebody, I says. If Hondo tried to scratch hisself he tore the blood from hisself, if he tried to open somethin he tore it all to pieces, if he . . . well finally it was like he was tied all up in ropes or like he was a frozen man he was so ascared to touch somebody. Pore Hondo had so much soft lovingness to give to everbody but he did not know *la mensura,* what you call it, measure? He did not know one pound from one ounce. What was pore Hondo going to do? Sometimes if he opened a door he pulled it down. Lots of things was broken around him. What was Hondo goin to do? And people wouldn't come too close to him, what was he goin to do? He was in the worst jail of all, I told him, worse than anything in Missoura or in anywhere I told him, all locked up. But what am I goin to do? Hondo asked me. I will help you Hondo, I told him. Through *Jesucristo* who helps everbody and everthing. And I told Hondo about the blind man that He made to see and the deaf man and the lame ones to walk—*los ciegos y los sordos y los cojos.* How will *Jesucristo* do it? asked Hondo. We will ask *Jesucristo* to make you *suave* gentle, I says. *Jesucristo* I prayed please to make Hondo *suave,* Hondo, a gentle man who does not know his own *fuerza* strength. And *Jesucristo* give me back the message—steal the curl of hair from Hondo. What? I says. What? asked Hondo. Nothin', I says. But now I knew that *Jesucristo* was *La Médium,* the Medium that was giving me the message that would save Hondo's *mi compadre's* life. And so one night when Hondo was asleepin, from his open hand that had fallen open in his sleep I stole the Bull Durham little sack that held the hair and hid it in my breast. When he woke up he was already so *suave* gentle that he resigned himself to the precious loss and for a long time cried just like a baby. But we went on and Hondo now was such a soft man that lambs run to him in the fields and even a butterfly sit on's shoulder onct, twas far in Oregon and the butterfly was yellow.

And his *abrazos* was as soft as Jesuses must have been. Hondo seemed just like a saint. Sometime he cried again to lose the little curl but we went on and sometimes more than ever now he cried for Sweet Janine that he had never meant to choke to death he only was alovin her and did not know his own strength. I did not go to, I did not go to do it! cried pore Hondo Holloway. But we went on. We slept against each other in the fields and when the frost fell over us we held each other keeping warm and it was just as tender. But in all our tendernesses never did I reveal myself to Hondo.

In every town we come to, Hondo Holloway would go to the Mayor's place and read down the list of people of the town to find Johansson. *En fin* in one town there was Johansson. Hondo said there is the little Savings and Loan Bank this is the bitter town of Sweet Janine my heart is heavy and bitter. Never mind I says to Hondo when you have made forgiveness amends to Ethelreda your bitter heart will not be so heavy. But of course it will always be a little heavy and still a little bitter until you dig back up the money under the Missoura jail and give it back to the Savings and Loan Bank of this town. One thing at a time please Arcadio, answered Hondo, first the forgiveness amends. When we went to the door and big Ethelreda opened it and *suave* Hondo said to her who he was, with one blow of her big hand she killed him down to the ground and I run for my life. *Jesucristo* I called out, save the soul of Hondo Holloway and forgive me for stealing the curl of hair I was only following the message that you give to me, what is this world? Pore Hondo Holloway. Oh God and *Jesucristo* I do not understand the working of your ways sometimes *señor*, with *fuerza sin mensura* Hondo murdered accidentally and *suave* he was knocked down dead.

I went on, all alone again, trying to figure out now who I was ahunting for and seen again that was, as always, as in the beginning, my mother. You wan hear? And when something tickled on my breast oh my God and *Jesucristo* twas the little curl of hair of Sweet Janine that first was carried by Tomasso that Hondo give him and now twas in my care.

Feelings for the Show come over me again and I wondered should I come back to the Show. And I looked again for posters on the trees with great head of a lion *feroz*, Heracles, and in the towns I went through asked the people if they had some *noticias* of the Show but nobody did.

12

The Missoura Jail

HE THOUGHT WAS
beginning to occur to me—thought it twas a thought but
as I thought about it more I begun to see that it was God
and *Jesucristo*'s thought athinkin for me—the thought
was to go towards the Missoura jail. I would take the curl
of hair back to Old John, tell Sam Policheck, the jailer,
that Chupa was my mother and that I was the half blood
brother of Tomasso that he brought up when his mother
left him, and dig for the Savings and Loan that Old John
would show me where, return it to the little Savings and
Loan Bank in the bitter town of Sweet Janine and so
clean the bitterness from the heart of Hondo Holloway
and get him into heaven—not *Virgen's* Heaven because
of Gloria Ox and I don't know what others. Then I was
sure that God and *Jesucristo* would forgive the sins of
Hondo Holloway. This was my mission given to me by
God and *Jesucristo* in my thoughts. And I would see the
old Missoura jail where all those that I loved had all been
at one time or another! You wan hear. And I could ask
some information from Sam Policheck about *mi madre*
when she was a prisoner there for stealing a green dress

with sparkled fringe and ask Nan Policheck about Tomasso and his jail cell school and try to make amends of
forgiveness for Hondo for digging the hole of excape. So I
was agoing on towards Missoura.

I walked through towns and slept in sheds and under
bridges, headin for Missoura. I was full of joy that I was
goin there. Since I was on the mission given to me by
God and *Jesucristo* in my thoughts, they looked after me
and led me on, you wan hear. *Feroz* dogs come after me
in some places and in a valley of a place I don know the
place some *ladrones* robbers fell upon me and tried to
beat me but I had great strength like *Santo Pablo* Paul in
La Biblia Blanca, and I repulsed them, like *La Biblia* says.
And I went on, towards the Missoura jail. There was great
rains in some mountains, I don know where, and I was
drenched and freezin cold but then the sun come out and
dried me off; and I went on. And findin myself in a whole
bunch of little black bullfrogs just coverin the whole
ground one time, I run up in a tree and set there all one
night and oh the groanin of those black bullfrogs was so
terrible to hear, *demonio;* but in the morning they was
gone and I went on, towards the Missoura jail.

And so I got to the Missoura jail in the very foot-
steps of God and *Jesucristo* that led the way. Where is it?
I asked them when all I saw was houses of a town. Look
yonder I thought I heard God and *Jesucristo* my leaders
say. And there was the Missoura jail, up behind the MKT
rayroad depot. When I knocked on the door, a man
opened it and he had white lips and a cap that looked like
a miner's cap and the man was lopsided because of a ring
of heavy keys ahangin at his groins. I said I am a friend of
Old John's and have come to see him. Then you better
hurry, says the man, because Old John is breathin his last

breaths. Please take me to him before he breathes the last one, I says. And the man says are you a priest? And I says I have come because of the thoughts of God and *Jesu-cristo* and my name is Arcadio what is yours *Señor?* And said Sam Policheck. The Bohunk, I thought but did not say it. At last I have found you, I said, Sam Policheck. I have many things to ask you and to tell you. If you want to see Old John with still some breath in him, said Sam Policheck, then you'd better not make small talk and hurry back to his cot in the cell where he has been confined for many days since the excape of Hondo Holloway through a hole, which has exhausted him to death to help dig. I am not making small talk Mr. Policheck, I says, and we can be friends for we have much in common and I have many things to tell you and many questions to ask. Where is the hole that Old John dug for Hondo to excape in is one question. All cemented up, it is now a hole of pure Instant Cement and the same hole that Tomasso went out through says Sam Policheck, but if you expect to see Old John abreathin I'm tellin you we better hurry. To the confined cell under the ground because of two excapes that he assisted in.

When we got to the confined cell I asked Sam Policheck to please to give me ten minutes alone with Old John and Sam Policheck said, you'll be lucky if you get two because I don't believe he has that many left. And there was sweet Old John all silver with a beard all over his breast and silver hair aflowing over his shoulders. You are a prophet from *La Biblia* I says, and fell upon his silver breast and cried. Please hurry I don't have many breaths left before the last one, Old John said to me, who are you what have you come for what do you want? In a hurry I showed him the Bull Durham sack of Sweet Janine's hair. Old John cried and was so weak on his cot could hardly take the little sack in's shaking hand. And I told him of Hondo's tribulations and *desgracias* and of his death at the big hand of Ethelreda. And before Old John begun to breathe his last breath I whispered give me directions where is the buried Savings and Loan and where is the hole you dug with Hondo. Old John whispered me they filled the wrong hole with Instant Cement, look in the corner by the Rose a Sharon and these were his last words with his last breath, he died lovingly in my arms I had got there just in time. And then I looked up and saw on the wall all the names, saw Tomasso's homework of arithmetic figuring that he did when this cell was his schoolroom: $2+2+2=6$ and his little name scribbled T-o-m-a-s-s-o and saw *God Loves Me* and *Suffer the Little Children* when twas his Sunday School with Nan Policheck and saw the name of my mother C-h-u-p-a, mother and son names on the walls who never saw each other and saw H-o-n-d-o and saw O-l-d J-o-h-n and there I wrote my name Arcadio and wrote *has finally come here but too late*, you wan hear. And the salt of my tears would have rusted my face if I had not wiped them off. But I was stuck back with the curl of hair again, you wan hear. I will have to wait to hear the thoughts of God and *Jesucristo* to know what to do with this curl of hair I said. For one more minute, though, I sat and played my frenchharp music for Old John, twas "The Waltz of the Spotted Dog."

Sam Policheck come to the confined cell and says why are you playing "The Missoura Waltz," did you know that it is one of my favorites? I do not know what is "The Missoura Waltz" I says, what I was playin was an old song from the Show called "The Waltz of the Spotted Dog." Well it's "The Missoura Waltz" the very tune. This was news to me. Then I asked Sam Policheck if I could bury Old John in the yard and he said where do you have in mind and I says under the Rose a Sharon tree and Sam Policheck said that it was okay. Where is Nan Policheck your wife I asked Sam Policheck. Dead said Sam Policheck. And buried in the jailyard why do you ask?

And then I told Sam Policheck who I was, that is a friend of Hondo Holloway's and Tomasso's half blood brother and the son of Chupa the woman who stole the green dress, all former prisoners of the Missoura jail and under his lock and key and Sam Policheck threw me into the jail cell and locked the lock without one word. Oh God and *Jesucristo* here was I a prisoner in the Missoura jail! Like St. Paul that I have told you, you wan hear, and that then was an earthquake in *La Biblia* for to shake open the prison door and that there a basket was let down to him. Oh God and *Jesucristo* I called out, free me from the bondage like your son *Santo Pablo*. But right away come back Sam Policheck to my prison door and I said in my best words Mr. Policheck could I persuade you two things, one that you call a resident of the town Ethelreda Johansson to come out and be at the burial of Old John, and two to let me dig the grave for Old John like you earlier promised me. Okay, says Sam Policheck, you will be doing Missoura jail a favor before he smells. And use the lime we use, lime's out back in the shed. And that was how I found myself joyfully sliding through the blessed hole that once Tomasso got free in and when it was finally made big enough by Ethelreda's great big hand. I said Ethelreda you can help get rid of the sin in you for killing Hondo Holloway if you will come by night and help me with your big hands dig the old hole bigger so that I can fit into it. I am a big person. But first I'll dig, myself, the grave of sweet Old John. And when we'd put him in it made a cardboard tombstone out of a box top and on it wrote his name OLD JOHN.

Ethelreda said her confession of forgiveness amends to me, said she had been waiting for somebody to come to the town that she could make her amends with, said now she realized that she did not know her own strength like Hondo the very man she had wiped out with her big hand. Pore Hondo I says was wiped out by the hand of somebody didn't know their own strength just like him. Pore Hondo, says Ethelreda, I will do something in his memory, what would you suggest? Dig the hole bigger, I says. So she come by night and help me find the Rose a Sharon tree and then we found the beloved old hole that was first dug by Hondo and Old John to help Tomasso, then by Old John mostly to help Hondo Holloway, twas probably what caused him to breathe his last breath, then by Ethelreda's big hands to help me, Arcadio, crawl through where the others had gone. And I felt such great love for them that ud gone before me as I was acrawlin through, Tomasso and then Hondo Holloway that had crawled through and excaped into the world free. When I come out the end twas dark midnight and I was on a hill one way looking at a big town sparkling, other way down in the valley looking at Missoura jail where Ethelreda was now. Farewell I says farewell Missoura jail and in my arms the baitbox of Saving and Loan that according to Old John's instructions I had plucked up from the Rose a Sharon's roots that clutched it safely under the ground of Missoura jail. And the curl of little hair in the Bull Durham sack tucked against my breast. But oh my God and *Jesucristo* just as I come out the other side of the hole I heard great cries and twas Ethelreda, they had caught her. And now she would be thrown into the cell where all the rest of us had been. Sam Policheck had caught pore Ethelreda and now she would be his prisoner. Who would free Ethelreda Johansson I wondered as I started out for the bitter town of Sweet Janine with the golden baitbox—I will tell you why it was golden directly—of Savings and Loan. Those two pore sisters of that bitter town, I thought, one murdered accidentally and the other jailed for life as she was ahelpin out somebody else—me excaping through the old hole. One day I says to myself I will return to Missoura jail and try to bail out Ethelreda Johansson.

Well twas another journey this one towards the bitter town of Sweet Janine with under my arm the golden baitbox that had turned to gold from rust of the Rose a Sharon. Twas not always under my arm twas sometimes between my legs as I laid asleep at night for fear of *ladrones* thiefs. The Rose a Sharon tree had given such a sweet smell to the baitbox that the sweet smell followed me all day long and twas sweet in my nostrils all night long. I am the Rose a Sharon like the Bible says about *el rey bello* the beautiful King Solomon. The baitbox was so golden with rust of the roots of the Rose a Sharon and the golden rust had locked it up forever looked like, God knows what kind of a bank can open it, I says to myself. But on I traveled with it. I did not dare to ask *noticias* of any bank where a bank of savings and loan would be in the towns because I would be beaten up and robbed and thiefs would run off with the golden baitbox, so I could not ask *noticias*. But I tried to follow the same path to

Sweet Janine's bitter town that I had traveled before. But town was achangin so fast, whole buildings fell and other ones rose up before you could get to Missoura jail and back to where you come from. Ethelreda had told me that her and Sweet Janine's bitter town could be seen for a long ways on the road by noticing a swarm of black rathawks over a certain place. These rathawks was ahuntin for a very famous pack of smart rats, white and nobody had ever heard of a white rat before, that had lived in that town for many many years and could never be caught in any trap or killed in any way, they were the most smartest rats ever known—and *white*, you wan hear? The bitter town of Sweet Janine had put this circle of black rathawks in the air over the town to keep out an eye. Everbody keepin out an eye, you wan hear, even rathawks. These black rathawks were treated like kings and queens by the town and was given everthing that they would want, pure beef and pure whipped cream and artichokes for some reason these black rathawks liked artichokes and this bitter town had to send for these artichokes. This is what they told me. These black rathawks was always in the air, their circle was never broken night nor day, no one ever saw the circle broken, old old men that had grown up in the bitter town from children said that they had never seen the circle broken. How do they rest? I asked one of these old old men. Who knows? answered the man. At night the rathawks called to let you know that they were there. The nightcall of the rathawks over the bitter town of Sweet Janine was a terrible sound to hear, *demonio*; and when I first heard it I says this town is a bitter town. You wan hear? Which one was the pride of the bitter town I asked a person of the town, rats or rathawks. I do not know, said that person, they are both world-famous. Well I have never heard of them before I got to this town, I says. That's because you do not know anything, this person says to me. To give you an idea of how bitter this town was.

The Bitter Town of
Sweet Janine

SO I KEPT OUT AN EYE
for a circle of birds. And suddenly up ahead of me one
mornin I seen what I knew was the bitter town of Sweet
Janine because there was a circle of birds over it. These
must be the famous rathawks keeping out an eye for the
famous smart white rats. And then night fell black on me
and asleepin in an old shed I heard the terrible calls of the
rathawks all night long and I shivered and thought this is
a bitter town. Next mornin I went straight to a sign that
says SAVINGS AND LOAN and in there I returned the
golden baitbox of money to the Savings and Loan bank
personally to the President named Fred Shanks. Would
you possibly be kin to a Shanks that used to run a Show? I
asked this President named Shanks. My distant cousin,
said President Shanks—real distant, never met the crook
that used my name on a bunch of hot checks and almost
reduced the surplus of this Savings and Loan Bank to a
zero. The police was after him but they never caught him.
Oh my God another posse, I says, and this one after Old
Shanks—there was a posse out after everbody, a posse
was ahuntin the hunters that was afleein the posse, soon

there would be a posse hunting a posse. What is this world, you wan hear. But in all my runnin and huntin I was yet to see one posse.

This President Fred Shanks told me about the *desgracia* of the Show. That the Show was gone. That the Show was fallen into ashes on the ground from a terrible fire caused by a rampage of Heracles the Lion that after all the years suddenly got back his *feroz*, Heracles become again *feroz* as he was in his old wild days before the Show and leapt up on Old Shanks and tore out his throat and then tore off his old balls and pulled aloose his arms and tore him to pieces and the Show caught all afire and burned down to the ground, everthing. But where is Heracles the Lion? I asked. At large, said the President. All the towns are keepin out an eye for him and there are a dozen posses. What is this life, what is this world, I says, My God and *Jesucristo*.

And then Fred Shanks pulled out a newspaper story of it and said that there it told that a Dwarft was almost a hero fightin to the last the terrible conflagration with big buckets of water twict as big as he was until, newspaper said, the fire got him. They found him kneeling in a shape of prayin and when somebody touched him said a whole Dwarft fell into ashes on the ground. My God a whole Dwarft of ashes. What is this world? But looked like Eddy the Dwarft prayed, he must have remembered my *Biblia Blanca*, that I told him and he wouldn't listen but I guess he did guess that some of *La Biblia* got into his little Dwarft ear 'bout as big as a snail. Must've prayed, little Mescan Dwarft Eddy Gonzales that said he was an atheist. God save his lonesome little soul. I'll remember him a minute now, in this afternoon; but he was still a mean little codger. You wan hear?

WILLIAM GOYEN

The piece of the newspaper that the President Fred Shanks showed me did not mention nowhere the gilded chair or the jewel wagon. Guess they're ashes too. Shanks give that golden chair to me when I was young I'd seen him nailin and sawin something secret many days, said twas a secret what he was amakin and then seen on his fingers gold, seen gold; and then he called to me one night to come and see and twas the chair of gold. Set in it, he said, go on set in it and I was ascared at first to set in something gold like that; but Shanks got hold of me and carried me in's arms, gentle then, to the chair and sweetly set me down, into the golden chair. And twas lust of me, *lujuria,* that made him do it, *lujuria,* lust that made him build a chair of gold. I saw some tears, I'm pretty sure, in Shankses eye. Thank you Shanks, I said, and I felt good then do you hear, *Oyente?* Wouldn't you, if somebody'd give you that and 'd built on it and built on it; wouldn't you? Felt good? So Shanks I'll remember a minute right now in this afternoon under this old trestle that you told me that you loved me that one night long ago in the jewel wagon, called me your *joya morena,* Mescan words I told you, means a dark jewel, a jewel in a jewel wagon that you bought for me, you said. And oh I guess I got to remember that there uz times when you uz gentle with me *suave* and I'll 'member them for just a minute too, before I forget you forever; and I remember so many times I saw you so *feroz* of me in jealousy and that I saw you take a knife at me to keep me all your own if I should have a feelin' for another; even for the Dwarft you took at knife at me to make me swear to you he never touched me and I swore to you I never let him touch me, twas a lie Old Shanks my God I've had one half the world of Satan on me why should I turn down one pore Dwarft to learn

God's Bible? You wan hear. And so I say to you *Oyente*
that I have to give just one warm thought for Old Shanks
again right now here before you as you listen: he half lost
his sad mean mind for me and I have seen him beg me
beg me just to say I love you. I forgive and I make amends
of my forgiveness to lost Shanks, especially for the chair
of gold which even then could not make me say to Shanks
I love you, not even for the jewel wagon that he give me,
this was in the early days when I was young and come to
him to get a job with the Show you will remember
Oyente how I told you, how I revealed myself to this man
Shanks out in the fields when I was young and run away
from the *China Boy* do you remember? *Sí*. Now I want
to say before God and *Jesucristo* and before you *Oyente*
that I forgive and make amends of my forgiveness to lost
Shanks. But when he saw that he would never have me all
his own that is when his mind got mean on me because
he couldn't have me, onct I took a piece of glass, of a beer
bottle, and put it at his lips to harelip him if he would try
to touch me once I slept with a great big rock beside my
pillow that I would bash in's head if he come at me in my
sleep and in some nights I'd wake up when the little dog
barked—bark 'bout as big as a little bitty mouse—and see
at the window Shankses face, *demonio*, of wanting my
body while I slept naked on my bed it was so hot in that
jewel wagon. And one terrible night I felt him on me in
the dark I thought twas a hot animal from the Sideshow,
wet and hair and hot and quiet and with my piece of beer
bottle under my bed with my piece of glass I cut his lip
and give him the scar on's lip forevermore until he died
by the *feroz* of Heracles the Lion, hairlipped, Shanks had
the sign of's lust, *lujuria*, of's madness over me cut upon
his lip, he'd been *cut*, a little pink curl on's lip that he'd

run his tongue on, over and over, twas a sign of his madness and I knew it; and he never come at me again. Old
Shanks.

About the story of the newspaper what was the
name of the town I asked this President Fred Shanks and
he said I don know, newspaper does not give name of the
town. But who cares the name of the town said Fred
Shanks you are apprehended hereby for robbery of a Savings and Loan Bank. How do I know who somebody
named Hondo Holloway is, he said, *you* had the money
on you! And President Fred Shanks threw me into jail in
this bitter town.

But what had happened was that over in the Missoura jail Ethelreda had told Sam Policheck of her killing
of Hondo Holloway with her big hand when he come to
beg forgiveness, for the murder of her sister Sweet Janine.
And God and *Jesucristo* helped Ethelreda sweeten up her
nature and beg forgiveness for diggin the hole bigger for
me and helped her talk to Sam Policheck about excaping
through the hole away from Missoura jail and into the
world. Your wife Nan Policheck has been a long time deceased said Ethelreda, and I would like to free you from
your own jail. World outside has got a lots that you don
even know about. Includin me, added Ethelreda. So
would you understand that there was Sam Policheck
ahelpin dig the hole bigger—for himself—and for Ethelreda! And one night Sam Policheck followed Ethelreda
through the hole that he had helped make big enough;
and they both come out into the world free and both full
of forgiveness and glad that they was free and wanting to
make amends to all of those that had been thrown into
the cell of Missoura jail by Sam Policheck.

First thing that I have to do, Ethelreda says to Sam

Policheck, Ethelreda said, is make forgiveness amends to Hondo Holloway. How can you make amends to a dead man asked Sam Policheck, Ethelreda said he said. Take him off of the cold stone slab at the Morgue in the terrible town where I lived, says Ethelreda; and where he has laid ever since I struck him the fatal blow. So first thing they done, this excaped couple and the last ones of all of us to leave the old Missoura jail and to board it up forever, since the town was plannin to open up a new one in a shoppin center it was goin to build next to a cultural center it was goin to build, somebody said; meantime all crooks run free in the town; first thing they done was to head for the bitter town where pore lonesome Hondo laid cold dead on a slab of stone all this time without a livin soul to claim him with a sign on him that said PERSON UNKNOWN. And to take off the sign and carry him back to boarded-up Missoura jail and bury him there under the Rose a Sharon where so much had been buried—Old John and the golden baitbox of Savings and Loan to name two. What are the others? I don know guess I was exaggeratin. No I wasn't because Nan Policheck was buried in that jailyard too but not under the Rose a Sharon. Anyways Ethelreda laid Hondo Holloway in the ground of Missoura jail under the bloomin Rose a Sharon tree that always was abloomin, never anybody saw ever that sweet little tree 'ithout a blossom on it. Old ground'd been dug up so much just opened up on its own before Ethelreda when she lifted up her great big hand, didn't even have to dig, ground just opened up to take body of Hondo Holloway in it, seemed like he was home. This's what Ethelreda Johansson told me.

So big Ethelreda made her forgiveness to Hondo Holloway by diggin with her own big shovelin hand, the

WILLIAM GOYEN

very one that struck him down to death, iz grave. And
next to the grave of Old John where the cardboard tombstone made of a box top said OLD JOHN printed long ago,
whenever it was, when was it my *Oyente* do you know?
can you follow all the years and all the happenings that
I've told you, how many years? how many things happened? What is this world *Oyente?* You wan hear. But
now I felt better about my friend Hondo cause I knew
where his grave was and said that I'd one day go back to
the Missoura jail to put flowers on it. But guess I didn't
have to since I'm sure sweet Rose a Sharon tree dropped
flowers enough on it night and day, flowers on the grave
of Old John, too.

And one night when there was heard a big esplosion
in the bitter town of Sweet Janine the jail door of mine
opened like in *La Biblia Blanca* like in *San Pablo,* and
when I run through the open door I found Ethelreda and
Sam Policheck arunnin through the streets, we was in a
reunion together! God and *Jesucristo* had brought us together again in a miraculous, in a *milagro.*

Why have you returned to this bitter town? I cried.
And with my God Sam Policheck the *Bohunk.* I says this
Bohunk out loud to him this time after what he had done
to me, thrown me into Missoura jail. Everthing has
changed all the past is forgotten and all is forgiven by
everbody, cried out Ethelreda. And when I says I hope
that includes pore Hondo Holloway that come to you in a
pure heart and you wiped him down out of his life, pore
Ethelreda Johansson cried biggest tears I've ever seen,
they fell on the sidewalk of that bitter town like pancakes.
You could hear her big tears flop down on the sidewalk. I
was ascared a little, to see such a great big person acrying
like that; and then she told me what I have just told you,

about her amends of buryin Hondo Holloway off the cold slab into the blessed ground of Missoura jail that opened up to take him in. I'll go take flowers to iz grave she cried. Please, said Sam Policheck. Not back to Missoura jail. Although I second everything that is happening, said Sam Policheck, a very changed man. Nan Policheck was a little woman a good woman and a good little wife for a jailer, said Sam Policheck. But a little woman. Now I have me a good big one, Ethelreda Johansson, and everthing has changed I am no longer of a jail and have boarded it up and buried the keys under the Rose a Sharon by the hole of everbody's excape, said Sam Policheck. We have come, said Ethelreda right into what Sam Policheck was saying, for me to get a few of my things before the *desgracia* hits the town. Well I have just excaped from the jail of this town because of a terrible injustice of a President Fred Shanks but a mysterious esplosion busted open my jail door and I am at large again, I said.

The mysterious esplosion was a part of a warning, said Ethelreda, that there is about to begin an infernal battle to the death between rathawks and rats, we have for a long time known this would happen it was even prophesied by a famous Medium. What was the Medium's name? I asked. How would I know? answered Ethelreda. I thought it might be Gloria Ox, I said. But Ethelreda went right on into what I was sayin. Medium, Ethelreda went on, said that it will be preceded by a mysterious esplosion and a bloody battle will demolish the whole town forevermore. That is why I have returned to get a few things. Let em demolish it, I said, it is a bitter town. A town of nastiness, said Ethelreda, excuse the word but it is a nasty town. What happened to you in it?

I asked. I have never told my story, said Ethelreda. Now that the town of my life is about to be demolished, I think I will. You'll have to be brief, said Sam Policheck. I'll hurry, she said. We were two sisters in a nasty town. Bitter, I said. Please, said Ethelreda. I have only a few minutes and my time is limited. My sister Janine and I suffered at the hands of a nasty town. That is a *gringo* espression, I said, that a town would have hands. Please, said Ethelreda. My time is limited. They were always, since we were just girls, trying to take advantage of we girls. Who? I asked. The town, said Ethelreda. I may, she said, not have to tell this if I continue to be interrupted and with such a limit on my time anyway, because of the coming any minute of this town's demolishment, as history and the Medium decreed that it would. *Gott!* said Ethelreda. It was the only time I ever heard her speak foreign. What does that mean translated? I asked Ethelreda. Not into Mescan but into Anglo. God said she. In Swedish—or German, I can't remember—we are Swedish, or my father was, with some German thrown into it. My mother Innisfree was Irish—so I am part Irish and part Swedish with some German and my mother had some Scotch in her so I have that, too. I hate to rush you, said Sam Policheck, but only to remind you that time is limited. I'll hurry, Ethelreda said. My father Hans Johansson ran the oldest bakery in the terrible town. He made the best bread in Texas, up every morn to bake it in a four-o'clock oven. The only sweet thing about the nasty town was that the smell of bread was being smelled by the people before dawn. But . . . I said. Please, cut in Ethelreda. I was only going to say, I said, that if the people of the terrible town were so nasty why was it good that they smelled your father Hanses bread every morn? He should have laid out a nasty smell over that nasty town. *Please!* cried Ethelreda. When I have such limited time! cried out Ethelreda, almost raising up her big hand. *Perdóname Usted!* I said. *Señora. Señora* Ethelreda Johansson Policheck. A beautiful name, Sam Policheck put in. But Ethelreda went on with her story. But my father was treated so nasty when somebody found an unmentionable object in a loaf of rye that he was forced to close down his ovens. The whole nasty town treated him like a dog and tried to run him out of town. What was the object in the rye? I asked. An unmentionable object, answered Ethelreda, but an object that is supposed to keep you from having babies. Which set the town against each other, two sides, those in favor of sexual pleasure and those in favor of just having babies. A condom said Sam Policheck. My God, I said. Who won, which side won? Please, said Ethelreda. My father Hans was forced to run out of the nasty town. What about your mother? I asked her. My mother Innisfree? said Ethelreda. Locked us up, we two girls, in our house and run out of town with my father Hans, saying that they would be back. But they never come back. So we were two girls waiting for some help. One sweet one and one great big one I says to myself. Who come with the help? I said to Ethelreda. Hondo Holloway, she said. O my God, I said. How did Hondo get there? Hiding out from some people who were after him, said Ethelreda. By a lake outside the town Hondo had pulled a man's arm out of its socket and the people were after him. He was only trying to help up the man because he had fallen into the lake and was adrownding. Hondo was so surprised by what he had done, that the man was crying out in pain from the arm that was pulled out and dangling, Hondo was so mixed up that he jumped into the lake, just where the man had been, and tried to drown hisself. Ethelreda said Hondo said. You wan hear. He did not know his own strength, *la mensura,* how to measure his own strength, I says to Ethelreda. Like me, said Ethelreda. *Sí,* I says. But pore Hondo Holloway died from it. I told you how much forgiveness I have given Hondo Holloway, cried out Ethelreda. How much amends can a woman make? she cried out, pore murderer. *Perdóname,* I says, *Señora,* escuse me. God knows, went on Ethelreda, how Hondo excaped from the lake and got into our basement which was so boarded up by our father Hans and our mother Innisfree Johansson. But we found him one morning. Janine did. My sister Janine. Sweet Janine! I says. Ethelreda said that you might as well to have a white butterfly in your house as to have Janine her frail white sister in your house. Sometimes said she thought a white scarf like a veil was afloatin around her and twas Janine; or said if you would think of in your mind's eye—we have no such espression—of a petal of a dogwood then that would be Janine; said she was a white saint said she was pure snow. Sweet Janine! I said and thought of Hondo Holloway that loved and killed her but didn't even know that he was doin it. I am having to rush my words, said Ethelreda, so I will rush on. So we had a nice life in the boarded-up house me and Janine and Hondo Holloway; that is, until . . . I am feeling the beginning shudder of the demolishment of the town! panted Ethelreda. And suddenly before she could say us any more of her story there was a terrible sound more than I can say to you, twas *demonio,* and we run, me and Ethelreda and Sam Policheck, out of the town that was beginning to be torn to pieces by the infernal battle of the rathawks and the white rats. And before we parted again, never to get to hear the rest of Ethelreda's story, I give to Ethelreda Johansson Policheck back the little curl of hair that once was Sweet Janine's and everbody forgive everbody once again and then run on their way to excape the fall of the bitter town.

I run on, and up on a hill I looked down and saw like of the evil cities of *La Biblia* flames and esplosions of the terrible destruction wrought by the rathawks and the rats and heard, even over the esplosions, the *demonio* cries of the rathawks shrieking over the bitter town of Sweet Janine.

And I went on my way awanderin.

14

Song of Hombre

YOU ARE PERHAPS now asking for *noticias* of my father Hombre. Now while keeping out an eye for Chupa I now hunted Hombre my father whose nakedness I looked upon might have cursed me, I don know. And I guess I was still keeping out an eye for the Show, too. For Old Shanks that might not be dead and the glass wagon of jewels not broken, for any posters of the Show showing Heracles the Lion *feroz*, which was a lie but now was the truth. I kept all these eyes out. One day I asked myself, how many eyes I got? How many eyes I got to keep out for everthing? I'm blind with so many eyes out. That question ended, at that time, my hunting. I had out an eye for God and *Jesucristo* only. And I just went on at large telling my stories out of the White Bible, singing my song, *cantando*, to who would listen, a day for a day, a night for a night. And on my way to God.

I have no doubt that God sent me to where was my father Hombre, you wan hear? If you have stayed this long—the sun is falling behind the smokestack of what-ever kind of mill that is that smokes up the smoke that lays over this place. What kind of shit is that what kind of people would lay that shit of smoke over where they breathe, what kind of people?—if you have stayed with me then you will hear about my father Hombre. If you wan go, *Oyente*, the air, as I have told you, will hear, for I will finish this song that I begun. I see you are still here, *compadre*. I never asked you who are you? You must be something like me to have stayed this long—from morn to almost night—and to have heard with such *hospital-idad* my whole long song—well, not all, there are some parts that I left out. I must go into the bushes to let na-ture have its way but never mind I will go on singing from the bushes, *quizás* maybe you will want to do the same over yonder while you go on listening. Can you listen while you let nature take its course can you listen while you piss? Some people find it hard to piss and listen. Or to piss and sing. I do not myself have any difficulty pissing and singing. You wan hear. Who are you, who are you that comes here under this rayroad trestle without a rayroad, in this riverbottom without a river. My song must be filling your ear. You will have to sing it out your-self to get my song out of your head. Like Julius Hohen-steckel, man I knew where was it, I don know. Anyway, who are you, are you going to sing my song to someone else? I do not care, *compadre*, I sing to what ear hears. I have done my best to sing you others' songs, hope you will do as well, should you try to sing again this singer's song. I have heard, God knows, some others' song sung out so badly tongue of the singer should be tied, that is no song they sing that is no music. You wan hear.

My pore father Hombre was a Texas man, white not brown *como* like *mi madre* and he was borned around here by this river that once was. Since you have asked for *noticias de mi padre* or have you? cain't remember, Hombre is the Texas part of me, the one-half of my *mestizo* that my mother called it. Twas *mi madre* Chupa give me the Mescan as you will remember and lots of it, more than the Texas that my father Hombre give me. In my searching I come upon a man looked like my father. Twas in a tomato shed outside of Jacksonville Texas in the tomato season in East Texas, broiling August. Nothin like a ripe tomato of the fields in the sun of East Texas in the month of August. Twas not my father, but told me where to find a man said might answer to me.

Twas in a roomin house, then, that the man was, down in Houston, that this man in the tomato shed said might answer to me, *comprendes* you understand. If you are ahuntin somebody this is the way you have to hunt. So twas on Congress Avenue back behind the rayroad by the bayou, back in there, that I found him. How could this man answer I wondered because he was so drunk, sitting in a rocking chair with a blanket wrapped around him. Are you named Hombre? I said. No answer. Hombre? I called. No words. Hombre! I shouted. And the answer came, who are you looking for? Hombre, I said; my father. Where is your mother, he asked me. She run away again and I am again hunting for her. I would help you search for her but I cain't walk, knees still healing, said he and he pulled off the blanket and showed me the ugly knees. There was no more of Hombre after his knees. My God I said. Right said Hombre it was your God, twas certainly not mine, that took my two good legs, one day I'll tell you how. Oh I've eaten my bread in the sweat of my face. Can you buy me just a little shortdog of Red, I need me some wine. Hombre, my father! I cried. Sugarboy! Sugarboy! my father wept and hugged me to him. *Cuidado* I said, watch it. I was sure he was my father for I was familiar with that old grabbing hand, knew the feel of that old hand. And besides, how else could he have known my name. You never told me that you loved me, said my father. Well I never did I says to him, but guess I really never thought I did, but guess I always did, I says, and guess I do. And then my father Hombre grabbed aholt of me and hugged me and cried and I held him back just a little bit and said don't try anything funny like you used to. May the Lord Jesus Christ strike me dead if ever I was to lay one hand on you again, my father says. O.K. I says. And we hugged together and both cried. I have been hunting everywhere for you, Hombre said. But I was hunting for you, keeping out an eye everywhere, I said, what is this world where everbody is huntin for everbody and cain't seem to find them. Oh I looked everywhere, Hombre said. How could you look everywhere without any legs, with only two sore knees that haven't even healed. Well I looked before God took my legs, Hombre explained. My God I said what is this world.

Told me that he fell on the rayroad and train run over his legs but I believe it twas a woman got his legs. Everthing that happened to Hombre was a woman, you wan hear? I believe it twas a woman got Hombre's legs at the knees so he couldn't get away from her no more, so that he couldn't get on his knees over any other woman. Bet it didn't bother your long member, I said to him, that you made me with, like you used to tell me over and over. Wan see what made you, you used to ask me, wasn't God made you, was this, you used to tell me. Bet the rayroad didn't bother that, did it? I hope you will forgive me, Hombre my father said. Has been the curse of my existence, said, reaching for it. Don't reach for it, I said: I cain't speak in the Texas way my father spoke, I am too much Mescan from my mother Chupa to do that, but this is what my father Hombre said. I could see that he was worse than ever. With his great long member that had worn him down and made him tired and old and crippled without legs and sore scabbed knees that he couldn't get up on over a woman. But you sold me to the Chinaman I told him. We needed the money, he said. Hombre was still a sinful man of flesh, never known anybody like him, lived for his flesh, even with's two legs amissing, still an old flesh fiend. He was the sinful part of me, all my sin had come from that hell member that hung down from him. My joy and fear comes from *mi madre*, my sin of flesh comes from this man. I had to get that straight with him forevermore. See what I'm saying? he said. Three-legged man. See what I'm tellin you? Well I don wan hear that member talk again, I said; anyway it's whiskey talking, I said; get the tongue of that shortdog out of my ear, don wan hear whiskey talkin. It's wine, said Hombre. Red. Well bottle's got a tongue I don wan speaking into my ear, I says. Makes me think of Julius Hohensteckel, foul-mouthed individual once I knew, said Hombre. With's foul mouth pulled around under his left ear by a palsy—heard tell that it's the left ear the Devil whispers to us in—Julius Hohensteckel whispered to himself into his ear like a phone, his head was receiving the dirtiest things you could think of. Julius Hohensteckel had spoken so many foul words Lord one day just grabbed aholt of's mouth and pulled it around up under his ear and left it there for his lifetime. Buried him that way, mouth up under his left ear, 's widow Roberta Hohensteckel asked the funeral home if twas any way could set his mouth back where it used to be so that he would look the way he used to be, in iz casket; funeral director said cain't, impossible for a funeral director to do; said, Miz Hohensteckel is too tricky to work with, working with the mouth of a corpse is very tricky, 'slike trying to work the hole in somethin, how can you get aholt of a hole, can you feature that? the funeral director told the grievin widow Roberta Hohensteckel; he'd a said that to me I'd a told him to go work with iz own hole, smart-mouthed cocksucker talkin like that to a pore widow; and anyway, he said, people in the town wouldn't know who it was lyin in the casket, come to know his face so familiar with that lipless hole working and hissing up under the big flapped earlobe, said. The human mouth my ass! cried my father Hombre. Didn't stop Julius's dirty language one bit, his foul words went on apourin into his own ear, just beat his helpless eardrum with fucks and shits, whispered into his big bald windy head like a keg; plug iz ear or gag iz mouth, didn't matter, was always one open hole awaitin, if you plugged em both, ear hole and mouth hole, that brain blowin dirty words around probly would've tried to use iz bunghole to get em out. Julius Hohensteckel's brain boiled out foul words, spewed them into iz mouth and iz mouth spurted em into iz brain again. Like a fountain, I says. Saw one onct in a convent outside San Antonio where I hunted for word of my mother, fountain sprayed up same water over and over again, was its own beginning, comin from nowhere but itself, suck it in spit it out suck it in, over and over again, into itself, out of itself, bringin itself back to itself, dead water. I hate things like that, I said. What I was sayin, said my father Hombre, was not no convent what I was talkin about was Julius Hohensteckel with's mouth up under iz ear. Give himself his own ear. Could rim iz tongue into iz brain, said with iz tongue could feel iz brains, bunched like a cluster of grapes, said my father Hombre. My God I said, what an abnormality. Was a pervert said my father, I despise fuckin perverts. Who am I, I said to myself, who was Julius Hohensteckel who is this man before me what is this life? I'm gettin crazy I could go crazy. And I was going to get crazy and mad with my father like I used to and my old self was comin back and I was afraid I would get a streak going like I used to and that I would push him over to the ground, without any legs. All connected to my old wildness, wildness of words and wildness of feelings; and oh my *Jesucristo* many times wildness of deeds because sometimes in those old days with my father Hombre when I would get a streak I didn't give one flyin fuck. *Comprendes?* You wan hear?

Hombre told me that he just let his member lead him through his life day after day, was like a dog on a rope, said, old dog, been at me since I was nine years old, don know why I don jus cut it off and be shut of it. Why don you put it on the rayroad tracks and let the train cut it off way you said your legs was, I thought to myself, old flesh fiend. Pullin at me like an old dog, my father kept on, how could a man ignore a thing like that, wasn't no powder puff I'll tell you that, how'd anybody like to have a crowbar shove up between their legs all the time, big piece of iron between their legs all the time, like to drove me crazy, big crowbar. This is what Hombre told me cain't say it exactly like he said, you know, in's East Texas talkin, but that's what Hombre said. Hombre still scared me some, with's crazy orange wine eye when he got like that, don know what he would do to me, you wan hear, but I was ready to kill him if he tried some monkey business and if he showed himself to me, if he made me look upon his nakedness, the sin of Noah in Genesis 9 in the White Bible.

Said when he found me gone that day back in Shuang Boy's, he just let me go he did not send no posse after me, he just let me go. Where is Shuang Boy? I asked my father. Dead, my father answered. Of natural causes. What about *China Boy?* I asked. All to pieces, said my father. *China Boy* fell to pieces when Johna pushed the Chinaman down the stairs. But you said Shuang Boy died of natural causes, I said. Did, my father said, twas only natural somebody would kill an old crooked sonofabitch cocksucker rat like Shuang Boy.

Who is taking care of you without any legs, I says. Nobody but a woman named Johna, says Hombre. You mean Juana, I says. Johna, she says Johna, Hombre said. O.K. I says, where's Johna? And he says she'll come around directly, and sure enough there come Johna at that time. My God I says to myself that's Johna one of the *China Boy* women, the one, if I remember correctly, that first took me down with her, that taught it to me. Johna, I said, gazing at her, how is my father doin, thank you for taking care of my father. How you doin, said Johna, where you been we hunted everwhere for you. Everbody huntin for everbody, I says. And nobody finding anybody, or stayin for very long when they do, I says. You haven't changed much, said Johna, bet you just like you always was, and her eyes went down to my groins. Well my father has changed very much I said to Johna, my God one third of him is missing since I last saw him. His best part is still here, says she. Would I know anything else but what he's been tellin me ever since I arrived, I says. I didn't say to her how much she'd changed, my God, *una trucha vieja,* an old trout, she was of a reddish hair and swollen-looking mouth and had old dog's-ear breasts and a pair of dirty beads on and under her old dress was her blue thighs, spread a little and I saw between them, I saw her put out herself a little, old dog's mouth hangin, twas as natural for her to put out herself as twas for anybody else to lift their foot. Now I could see that Johna was there to do more than to just take care of *mi padre,* I saw what they was doing—Hombre was doing exactly what Shuang Boy had done those years ago that I told you about, you wan hear, Hombre was sellin old Johna like Shuang Boy did. Old three-legged flesh fiend, I saw no hope for him, my own father. Nor for Johna, but I didn't care, for she was not no blood of mine although I guess I did have a little soft feeling for her due to the early days of my going down with her first of all ever in my life with any woman, this was the first woman and you know what that feeling can be, *comprendes?* You wan hear? But I saw no help for my member-crazy father.

It was before my father that I opened up *La Biblia Blanca* and tried to read out to him, but he could not hear. He drank his Red and touched his big old member and mumbled words I could not hear to his long member and twas like another person he was amumbling to. Shades of the *China Boy.* When I requested him please not to do that he say don't you have no respect for what made you? Old dog. No, I says, you have not changed you are the same, got no memory except memory of flesh and lust memory you are cursed by your member. And only God and *Jesucristo* knows how much I hate to think of those old days and you the way you was, and that old Chinaman rat that sold myself to men and women before I could get a holt of myself and made me a fiend of the flesh—like you—until I run away and almost died with the suffering of *Jesucristo* until my own salvation come to me through the Father and Son in *La Biblia Blanca.* You are saying too much to me, Hombre said, for an old long-dicked stump-kneed man and belly full of Red. Johna go get me another shortdog or somebody go get it. I remember Sugarboy when you never slept or even eat much, just *fucked,* said the old three-legged fiend, said the poor lost *esclavo* slave to his own member, you couldn't get enough of any of it, says Hombre, never slept or even eat much, just *fucked.* My father growled that word, it was the sound of a dog, *feroz,* and *demonio* and you will please to forgive the word from my mouth but I say what my damned father said. I saw that terrible picture again before me, that *figura,* of us, that beast *feroz* of hair and flesh hunching and ahunching and ahunching and ahunching. *Chingada!* I cried. Whored! And I run upon my father and was ready to choke him blue and push him over to the ground. But God held me back and I said I forgive you, Hombre, dick-poisoned *padre,* dick-sick Hombre, I turn you over to God and *Jesucristo,* Father and Son, do you hear me, I forgive you. Johna gazed at me with old eyes of a serpent and put out herself a little to me and showed a little more of it to me. I held my *Biblia* against my heart that was beating so hard could have knocked open the doors of St. Paul's prison that he excaped out of in a basket or who was that, was that St. Peter, or when an angel come with a key and opened the prison door; or was it an earthquake—so many stories in *La Biblia Blanca,* cain't get em straight—was it an earthquake that shook the prison and shook open the doors of the prison and broke off chains of the prisoners. And the jailer woke up and saw the prison shook open and tried to kill himself with his sword because he thought that the prisoners had excaped but Pablo Paul called out jailer do not kill yourself, because we are all here. *No te hagas ningun mal, pués todos estamos aquí.* We have not excaped. And then *el carcelero* the jailer come arunnin and fell down at Pablo's feet and said *que debo hacer para ser salvo?* What do I have to do to be saved? And Pablo answered believe in *Jesucristo* and you shall be saved. And so Pablo baptized the jailer and all his family.

You talk too much Mescan, said Hombre. Like your mama. But the point I says is that God was ahelping prisoners to excape like he helped me from the Show through the *figura* of my *madre* Chupa—God knows she was no *angel*—and like he helped my brother Tomasso excape through the hole from the Missoura jail. *Comprendes amigo?* You understand, *Señor, Señorita?* God opens doors and drops down baskets. Helped another time St. Paul excape in a basket that they let down to the ground from a jail. To them in jail that asks him for some help, God gives a basket. What are you now, a preacher? Hombre asked me. You come here to preach to me? and to save my dick-poisoned soul like you callin it, to save my dick-sick soul like you callin it? Your soul's the prisoner of your sexual member, I said to him. Do you want to be a prisoner? My long sexual member as you are now callin it is the best thing I have, as you will remember. Johna said escuse me I'm going to get a shortdog of Red for Hombre over at Sweeny Mack's. Why don't you get two shortdogs—or hell three or four, I don care, I'm going to be drinkin em said Hombre. So you won't keep havin to go back and forth to Sweeny Mack's. Can't get three or four, Hombre, answered Johna, until I do some work, my God what do you think I am a machine? This is a Hell couple,

I said to myself, you wan hear, I am down in Hell with these two. Hombre said he wanted to tell me of his earlier days and said guess any father wants to, to his son, to tell him about earlier days. To tell you of my earlier days, he says, when we was all in East Texas, at the peckerwood sawmill. Knew that there'd be a pecker in it, I thought. And I said to Hombre see there's already a pecker in it and you just started. 'S always a pecker in it, said Hombre. When I was a boy in the sawmill town, I had the longest dick in the town and probly the county, was clear to me at an early age. Hombre I says you are talkin about your member when you said you were going to tell me of your earlier days—so that I could have some information, some *noticias* of who I come from—but I ought to have known that that was all that he could talk about, his long member. What else do you have to talk about, I asked. What else is there to talk about when you have on you a very long dick that has been in charge of your whole life since your earlier days. Tell it to the Marines, I mumbled. What? my father Hombre asked. I said are you going to give it to a museum when you die? or maybe to a Sideshow? Hombre said, Sugarboy would you scratch stump of my knee, almost itches me crazy. No, I said. Johna will when she comes back from Sweeny Mack's. Why is she so long? Hombre asked. She's working for shortdog money, I told him. What do you think she is, a *máquina* machine? I saw my father's *esclavitud* slavery and saw that God had sent me, Arcadio, his own child to come and free him from his terrible *esclavitud*. How was I to do it was my problem. And to free my mind of that memory—that *figura* that was scalded on my brain. I could hear Hombre say in my imagination when she comes back we can all three have it liked we used to. And sure enough I heard him growl in that dog's voice, remember when we all three had it? And before me come again the infernal *figura*. Oh God I said, Oh *Jesucristo* I said, take from me this infernal *figura* of the past. Twas in that house on the wharf over the river, you remember, growled that voice, there was the three of us. We both had it at the same time Johna and me. I heard my father's voice, *demonio*, growling like a dog *feroz*. You went crazy. Then we changed around and the woman part sat on me and leaned back to let Johna come at the man part, squattin. I was under, coming up from under, and Johna was squattin, straddlin. Then you just went crazy and took charge, like a bull. You had it *all*. We changed around so much, everbody going after everthing, we was all three just crazy people, couldn't finally tell who was who or who was where. It seemed like we was *all* everthing. Never known anything like it. And we went on and on, night after night day after day, the three of us, over and over and over, *fucking*. You was puredee gold, pussy of gold and dick of gold, why did you run away, you belonged to me. And now I got no legs and can't get up over anybody and live on Red and limp as a rope, why did you run away? Morphodite.

I do not know what salvation come into me to keep me from killing my father Hombre. I should have known that twas *La Biblia Blanca* of God and *Jesucristo* in there, in that white sweet book. What I did instead of killing my father for lowrating me and of bringing before me the infernal *figura*, what I did instead of killing him was to turn my back to him and squat down and say get on my back. He did not say a word. I said Hombre, *Padre, Papá*, get up on my back and let's go. He did not say a word and got up on my back. I helped him to excape. I walked out of town with my father on my back, and the knobs of his stump knees grinded into my ribs. Don't grab so hard I cain't breathe for God's sakes, I choked out, let loose of me a little, old fucker, old member-cursed Hombre, old prisoner, *Papá*. We was quiet a long time until sundown, going along. Sometimes I felt the old hands of my father curl up around my neck, soft. Maybe he does love me I thought; his touch had loving in it. And a reaching, and I felt some tenderness and some salvation. But I heard my father's voice say where is my Red? I did not answer. Where is my wine? he yelled. How do I know, I said, what am I supposed to do? Get Red, said Hombre, and he was achoking me. Well I'm not Johna, I said. We went on. Hombre begun to shake. I was walking like somebody with Saint Vituses Dance. Hombre was having wine fits. I'm going to fall I'm going to have the Red Fits, get wine get wine, Hombre shouted, I'm going to shake off, is it an earthquake, can't hold on, stop and put me down and get me some Red. I squatted and Hombre shook off me like a bug, he shook in the dirt and dust flew and he tore off his clothes and then he whirled naked around like some kind of a bug and his head was back and his eyes was aglaring and red fume fuming out of iz mouth. My God his very breath is wine fume, I said to myself, arms thrashing wild and the dust comin up red and his long terrible member whipping up the dust and whipping at Hombre. I couldn't get near him this infernal *máquina* whirling and the great member whipping in the red dust. And he suddenly stopped still in the red dust. Hombre! I called. Hombre! He was dead in the dust, covered with red dust, member like a tail, he was piece of the devil looked like, whipped to death in the dirt by his infernal member.

I carried this piece of a red devil that did not seem

no longer the body of a man, my father, till I found a well with a bucket hanging, and I dipped up wellwater and washed the body of my quietened father washed away the red fume with buckets of wellwater. But I said to myself as I was awashin Hombre, no wellwater in this world can wash away that fume on his soul only the water of *Jesucristo* can wash that fume away wash him *Jesucristo* wash my father clean. I buried this piece of my father in a graveyard I found up a ways on the road, found a big concrete tomb that its iron doors was open, must have been an earthquake come and burst open the iron doors *come dice la Biblia*, as the Bible says. On the tomb was written the big name HORK which is a name very hard for a Mescan to say, Hork, but that was the name; and then the names Johanna, Johan, Linda Sue. Johanna Hork my God. I laid my father Hombre on a shelf in this concrete tomb and when I come out I saw twas an angel settin on the rooftop, an angel of stone, looked green in the light of the moon, a green angel over Hombre my father, the color of my mother Chupa's dress that night that I saw her onct more for a little while and I said to this green angel if you're Chupa I left your devil husband with's quietened member in the concrete room under you, 's member can't get you anymore cain't get him anymore what is this life green angel what is this world what is a mother what is a father?

At the gate to the graveyard was Johna waiting for me. Is he dead, she asked me. And dead I said. Thank God, Johna said, now I can rest. Where have you come from how did you know? I followed you, Johna said, with Hombre on your back, where else was I to go, please let me go with you. We went on, me and this first woman, woman that took me down with her long ago in the

China Boy. I guess I had this respect for her, a man never forgets the first going down. I could not at that first time understand the softness and the soft deepness, twas without a bottom no end to it; and the pain of it, am I hurting you I asked, this must hurt you. Baby, Johna said. And I never knew something like this. So you understand *compadre, Oyente,* you wan hear. Johna was *especiál* and even now somethin to be thought about, you wan hear. We went on. In a little ways farther we slept under a shed, twas a tomato shed, and when we woke up Johna was next to me and I felt warm in the dark her body was remembered to me as the early soft deep one of the *China Boy* and Johna says do you want some more of it? Of what, I says. Of what took you down for the first time at the *China Boy.* You mean at Shuang Boy's? I says. Yes Johna said, do you want to have it again, years later, hair of the dog of long ago. Old dog, I says. You and Hombre was the only ones I ever felt it with. Do you? she asked me. Do you, I said, want to have it again, some more of it, of what took you down for the first time, you was the first to have it from me back in Shuang Boy's. I don know, you wan hear, but I felt a wanting for old Johna and didn't even feel that I had to ask *Jesucristo* about it then and didn't even have the awful *visión* of the infernal *figura* now because of the third one of the *figura* my father Hombre was dead and his member put to rest, quietened by beating him down in the dust, his member had finally whipped him down in the red fume dust and he was laid up on a shelf in a concrete tomb of Hork with a stone green angel on the top, and there in the shed, twas a tomato shed, we come together, it had been so long but I just all unfolded and twas warm, not bad, bringing old *memorias* and seems to me now twas right for me to

WILLIAM GOYEN

132

come back so long later to that first woman, you wan hear, twas the end woman, twas the first and last, for me twas the *adiós* piece, and not bad, you wan hear, an old *máquina* still doing pretty good work. *Máquina*, I said, has held up pretty good. *Máquina*, what is that, asked Johna. Like a machine, something that works good. Well it's not a machine but it works good, said Johna. That's what I'm saying, I says. I did it, is all I know, says she. Like a lock, I said, like a lock takes and holds a key. I never felt much, you and Hombre was the only ones I ever felt it with, said Johna. You was just a more or less *más o menos máquina*, I says, for all those others. For the Red, said Johna, to get the Red for Hombre.

For the wine for Hombre, said she hid behind the factory on the bayou at lunchtime and took the men quick for a quarter. Back in the back, she told me, in the dark, the men from the factory got what they had to have, said. Go for a few days and then have to have it again. Tis a good business, can always count on it, can always count on men having to have it every few days, or for some every day. Like a *máquina*, I said. Guess everthing's got a *máquina* machine in it except God and *Jesucristo*. Whenever Johna went there to the factory, back in the back, no matter what time, day shift or night shift, when the wine money was needed, back in the back she would wait and always somebody would come, they would know she was there, they had to have it every few days, some of em every day. Men got to have it, said Johna. I did it is all I know. And then went with the money—proceeds is the *gringo* word, I says—and then went with the proceeds to Sweeny Mack's for the Red. For Hombre. Sometimes Sweeny Mack bought me the wine. How's that? I asked. With what I give him, Johna said. Oh I see, I said. Twas a direct change of the *máquina* for the wine. No money changed hands, she said. Why didn't you just stay at Sweeny Mack's and make the eschange I asked Johna, woulda been simpler wouldn't it, all in one place. Sweeny Mack, said Johna, liked to change money for what he got. Sweeny Mack wanted to see money. Didn't want to take the price of a shortdog of wine out in pussy. *Máquina* I said. I did it is all I know, said Johna. You could see that Johna didn't have many espressions.

And then I said Johna I got to go on, wherever I go you can't go with me. Where is that Johna said. I got to go on, I said. All right, go on, said Johna, but I hope you will remember me. I will, I says, you are the first one and the last. We had some times, said Johna. We had some times, said Johna, including the last one, Johna said; and I went on.

I felt so lonesome, now, *Señor, Señorita,* more lonesome than ever I have felt, ever in all my life of lonesomeness. Maybe because I had given the last of it to somebody, maybe because I had *finalmente* found my father, I don know. I felt many deep things as I went on, *Señor, Señorita.* I saw sights I wish I could sing to you, sometimes I felt my *mejicanismo* passing from me, I felt *everbody,* that I was *todo, all,* I felt great thoughts of the world, you wan hear? people fed me by the side of roads, I slept back in the fields and under the lonesome trees, I washed in rivers where there was some with water in em, and sometimes I walked all day in the dry rut of a river that used to be and felt the ghost of the waters sometimes could smell the vanished waters, that river-smell, nothing like a river's smell, I have many a *memoria* of a river, of the *presencia* presence of it in some nighttimes that I remember, sleeping by a river and the great *fuerza* of it, its force moving through the ground and the river smell guess I am part river, *Señor, Señorita, Corazón*, you wan hear. And great trees, holding deep in the ground I knew whole places of great trees, and the great *fuerza* of woods and great trees in 'em and their leaves, I love leaves, guess I am part tree, you wan hear? And I was movin along, I went on.

But in a little while come the old *máquina*, the old *adiós* piece, Johna again, Johna was waiting for me under a tree. I been thinkin that you need the *compañerismo* of a woman and hope that have changed your mind and will let me go with you wherever you are going. You and Hombre was the only ones I ever felt it with. Women do not seem to understand about *adiós* pieces, you wan hear, and about swan songs and always want to believe that there can be some more and they will use their *máquina* for this. I know, *compadre*. If you have the *máquina* you will naturally begin to deal with it, make a deal with it. I know, *Señor, Señorita*. You wan hear. I do not speak through my hat, as the *gringos* say. I am hunting for my mother I says to Johna. Well I am not doing anything especially, Johna told me. Now that Hombre is gone I would be glad to go with you and work for you like I worked for your father. I don't need no wine, I said. And no woman. Back there was our swan song, if that's what you would be planning, Johna. Try then to think of something, said Johna. You and Hombre was the only ones I ever felt it with. I can think of nothing, answered I. And I do not want to ever feel it with you again. I become mean and I am not sure why, I should have had pity for Johna that had lived all her life on her *máquina*, just like my father Hombre on his member. But I felt mean toward Johna and wanted her to go away, you wan hear. What do you want me to do? said she. I don wan you to do anything I found myself saying. Look, Johna said, and I could see that she was going to try to deal with me, to try to make a deal, naturally it would be a *máquina* deal because that is a woman's deal. Johna I said, don't try to make some deal with me.

Johna said saw very early about herself, that she had a *máquinita* little *máquina* and that if you had the *máquina* you would naturally begin to make a deal with it, said twas filled more often than her mouth but she never felt it much, said men filled her, taught her where she had what they wanted, taught her how to make a deal. Her mind was in her *máquina* from the early days, told me, her mind was on the deal. But she never felt it much, not until she was with Hombre and me. She come to the *China Boy* when she was sixteen years of age and had been there a long time when I got there, when Hombre brought me to old Shuang Boy Johna was already there. Said her name was Johna Katz and father's name was Grady Katz, never heard of him, owned a dry-goods store over at Lufkin Texas, Katzes Emporium, in the old days. And Johna was the first woman to take me down, and then with Hombre, they both worked me at the same time, and taught me and crazed me and locked me into them like a part of them like a part of a *máquina*, an infernal *máquina* of three pieces, and taught me and crazed me. The three of us was an unholy *figura* I told you about, twas a *fuerza* piece of human flesh aworking when we put ourselves together like that, fitted together like that, aworking, twas a *máquina*, an infernal *figura*. But I got free of that now, I said to Johna Katz, my father Hombre is dead, the third one is forever gone, and I am part of the river and I am part of the trees, I am no longer damned by the infernal *figura*. I said to Johna here, here is a stone, set on it. Set on this stone and look the other way, for I am going down the road and we will never see each other again, the infernal *figura* is gone. *Paz*.

I do not know whether Johna turned into the stone or not, but when I looked back I did not see Johna and the stone looked like twas shape of Johna. And so I went on.

15

Just a Little More
Before I Say So Long

B UT JUST A LITTLE
more. I heard tell of them finding in the deep swampwoods of the Looshiana bayou in the rainy season a dark
woman half eaten up by what was probably a great big
night hawk—some said a great big vicious owl would do
the same, that is attack and bite and claw to pieces a person so that you could not even tell of a face or of any part
of them much. Some bird *aficionados* that'd come in
there to the swampwoods to help wild birds brought this
news and said it could be the deed of some such bird
feroz, I don know. Of course I was ascared it might be
Chupa *mi madre* and remembered her all night, wherever
I was at the time I don know the name of the town. But
then they said again it could have been a man. Or could
have been the work of a devilish wild hog, or of a *demonio* coyote pack, or some wild swamp beast ascared of
a person suddenly appearing in the wild swampwoods. So
I did not pursue the thought that it might have been
Chupa, my mother, and hung my tears out to dry. I let
her go.

But why did not the *noticias* let me alone because

then there was some news of a woman *fantástica* that was putting on a big show in a filthy city in the East. She was sweetly dressed like a white angel and was walking a rope on her tiptoes across a *grande* dumpyard of garbage and did not fall or falter once and was called the Angel of the Dumpyards and was famous and was wanted by other cities and by Shows, yet she was not found again. She run away. Was that *mi madre?* You wan hear? And there was another runaway woman answering to the description I would give of Chupa run away with the richest young swindler in one part of the North and when they caught the young swindler with a million swindled dollars, the woman was gone and was not found again, bringing back to me familiar memories of Chupa my runaway mother. And a woman in a holy trance saw a picture of the Cross of *Jesucristo* on her screendoor and because of that begun to be able to heal people and to get presents from half the counties of Texas for a while; said the field in front of her house was crowded with cripples from half the counties of Texas. Until she run away and was not found again. Shades of Chupita, my *fugitiva* mother.

Yet I begun to hear tell of an old saint woman lived out in the bitterweed prairie back of the town that's over yonder, there in the prairie, and could tell the fortunes of people, past and ahead. I went back there and saw in the weeds of the prairie a little shotgun house settin under one shade tree, twas a big liveoak I believe. I knocked on the door that looked like hadn't been opened to anybody in a long time twas brambled over by vines that locked it. An old voice called me to come around to the front, and an old woman opened the front door and at first glance I thought twas surely Chupita. And then I wasn't sure.

From time to time I thought the old saint woman recognized me, a look in her eye at me. Yet then I saw I was mistaken.

Where did you come from I asked her, where have you been? My past is forgotten, the old woman said, it has been wiped out of my mind. Then you yourself need a person who can tell the fortunes of others, past and ahead, I said to her. Cobblers' children need shoes, she answered in a riddle. Is your name Chupa, I said. Tell me are you Chupa and were you once beautiful in a green dress of sparkled fringe? I was once beautiful the old *santa* answered me but I never to my memory owned a green dress, never wore that color. But said few come out here in the bitterweed prairie, who has given you *noticias* of me, and I said but everywhere it is said you are *una santa* that has an eye into the lives of others and does holy deeds of telling other people's fortunes. I have no such eye and I have never done no holy deed of fortunes, I live a *ermitaña* in this prairie of bitterweeds how could a hermit do a holy deed, the old saint woman said, since no one would ever know about it, the old woman saint said. You must have the wrong person. But I had such a hunch *Señor* that this was my mother and that if she could only remember, if I could only tell her her own fortunes she would recognize me her firstborn, Arcadio, the one she herself had told her own fortunes to, and I could come home, at last, and live in this house out in the prairie with my mother. That is, it seemed to me pretty sure that this woman of holy fortunes was *mi madre.* The thought to reveal my nakedness to her as once I did of yore years ago the night of my excape come *feroz* over me. But I did not, you wan hear, I did not reveal myself.

And so I give up again and let my mother-searching

go and went on my way towards God, looking for God, which don't need no help from anybody, nothing but yourself, don even have to take a step can do it setting down or laying down, that is the kind of journey looking for God is. This is what I begun to see. I hope He will show up soon. Meantime *canto*. I forgot to say don know why I have forgotten to say it or didn't remember to say it to you until now that the old saint woman in a moment of meanness looking at me with the *feroz* eye of a *demonia* threw me out of her shotgun house, turned me out with a strong arm, was unhospitable to me, showed me mean *inhospitalidad*. But I know that I myself have been a person of *inhospitalidad* many times back there in the Show, setting there still and without welcome, without *hospitalidad* to those standing before me and wanting to reach out to me—all but the unknown hand that reached out the White Bible to me, at which time I remember whispering in a voice that did not seem like my own, *Gracias*.

For a moment as the woman was throwing me out in her *inhospitalidad*, I wanted to turn and kill her—with a knife I do not know why I brought along for that possibility. I say surprisingly because as I tell this I am surprised that I would have such intentions and make such plans for *madre*-murder, knowing about the knocking, like it tells me—you know, to be still, to make *paz*. I only wanted to reconcile. But I saw how close *reconciliación* and *violencia* are to each other, *compadre*, those same feelings that are always in me, living together in my double person. The *inhospitalidad* of a woman who might be my mother was the grief I could not hardly stand no more, *no lo comprendió*, I did not know what to think, you'd have thought I was over those feelings now that I was seventy years of age—*creo que sí,* I believe—and had me some wisdom that come into me from the Show, from my mother's life and some from my father's, from the *China Boy,* from my long excaped life on the road living along the river in the earlier days and in the riverwoods where God fed me with a bird, a fish, a leaf, a berry, and slept on the ground or in trees. I did not see nobody for many days and many nights and then I was full of reconciliation and of *hospitalidad.* Or living outside of towns and cities sometimes going as a cowboy, sometimes in my uniform from some war I do not know what one, *quizás* a Mescan war perhaps, I do not know. Nor care. I came to doors and stood at back steps and asked for something to eat. Oh I have some wisdom of this life to give, *compadre, Oyente.* I have some opinions and some ideas. I am therefore surprised that I would have intentions to strike down a woman maybe was my mother. When she run away I understood, a little, you wan hear, *porque* I myself am a runaway and feel those feelings too; but to turn me out, to be turned away, was feelings only *Jesucristo* would accept from his own mother if he had had to but he did not; yet I had to, from a woman that might be my own mother, be turned back and I could not, I become *feroz.* I wanted very much to put the knife into this woman there in that place my mother one time showed me where my father Hombre once had printed on her *estómago* stomach underneath her how you say *ombligo,* navel, the little flower in the middle of the stomach: CHUPA with the letters wound in a little flowering vine. But I probably would not have found the CHUPA because the printing would have probably been rubbed off by all the years of rubbing that my mother put her *estómago* through, God knows. But *Señor* I did not put the knife.

You will say that *quizás* perhaps they would be looking again for me, if I had put the knife. As they did so long ago in the days of yore when I excaped the Show, under the invitation of my mother. I am sure those ones would not be hunting again for me, the old ones that old ridiculous posse. Then it would be the *policía* who would be looking for me, that is if the absence of the old saint woman was found out, if there was *noticias* of it in the town, I did not see any neighbors, only the old woman's house in a long field of blooming bitterweeds setting under the one tree, a live oak, I guess. And I would be at large again, excaped this time from *la ley* the law. Double at large, if I had put the knife, excaped from the Show and the Law.

And if they would be looking again for me then I could put on the woman's clothing and be there when they come for the unknown knifer and they would find the *milagro* miracle of the resurrected *santa* sitting in her bitterweed house. And no one would know that I had become my mother, *mi madre* Chupa. In this way, *Señor*, she could never run away from me again. And in this way would I find home and God and the end of all my hunting—for my mother, for my half brother Tomasso and for my dick-struck father. Do you say I should have done this, *Señor?* For if you would think that they would be looking for me I would not wait but go myself looking for them who was looking for me, to tell them of my deed and to ask forgiveness like *la Biblia dice que sí*, like the Bible says. That is, if it would be my mother. If twas not then I am sure that they would let me go in *paz*. And since there would be no way of finding out who was this woman that had had the knife put in her since the little flower would have had the little winding vine rubbed long ago away from it.

——■——

The fume of the dirty mill, my mother, my father, my brother Tomasso, all gone—*asunder* as it is the word in *La Biblia Blanca*, what, *Oyente*, would you now do? Would you go on down the road? Would you believe the newspaper story of Fred Shanks? Would you go on looking for the Show again, would you go asking people in the towns you passed if they had seen the Show, if'd been there, if there was any posters showing Heracles the lion *feroz?* Would you go back to the Show if you found it, back in the jewel wagon, back in the gilded chair before the silent gazers, still and silent evermore? Would you?

You, the listener of the singer's song, *Oyente*, who are you anyway? Why have you come this way and why have you stayed so long? I hardly see you now. *Oyente!* It gets dark and many stars come out in the Texas sky that my old ancestors Mescan and Texan saw, same sky same stars I do believe. And if you were to sing my song to another listener when my voice has stopped, how would you sing it to *your* listener, *Oyente*, would you be true to what I've sung to you, would you be careful not to add some of your own song to it what would be your song, *your* song, who are *you?* When I am silent. When I am gone into the night, into the darkness that has fallen all around us. I have seen that nothing lasts everything slips through your fingers, which is an espression. *San Pablo* said so. *La Biblia* tells me so, *dice que sí* on many pages. For, *Oyente*, if you will look you will see how the little white dog slipped through my fingers, how Chupa and Tomasso and Hondo and Hombre slipped through my fingers. Even the Show slipped through my fingers. *El Mundo pasa*. The world slips through your fingers. This leaves only God and *Jesucristo*.

The dark is here, *Señor, Señorita, Corazón Dulce,* hearer of my song, *Oyente. Qué más digo,* what more shall I say? *Qué más decir,* what more is there to say? For I am sure Old Shanks is dead and gone, torn to pieces like his brother said, and oh the little white jumper is surely too deceased, dust; and the Dwarft too, ashes, and the Show tent ashes on the ground I bet you money. God knows it was rotted enough even when I was under it, could see the stars through rotten holes in it and the wind, even back there, blew pieces of it like wild flags, many nights I heard in the quietness of my tent of gazing, the cracking of the wild flags in the starry wind. That leaves the last thing, God and *Jesucristo,* father and son, only thing that is the same today and yesterday and forever more. I'm on my way to them.

The dark is here. I'll take a minute to be quiet and play a little of "The Waltz of the Spotted Dog" for all them that I loved and for all that slipped through these old fingers.

It's time to say farewell and so goodbye *adiós* old world, old world is passing away. And so I say so long *adiós,* so long to all I loved and will not hunt for anymore, to Chupa, Tomasso, Hombre, Hondo, to all *adiós adiós* so long. And so long *adiós* to all the Show, Old Shanks and Eddy the Dwarft and the little white jumping dog

Junipero Perro, and Edna Pappas of *las palabras* and Heracles the lion *feroz* that found his old *feroz* again, so long, and to the gilded chair and to the jewel wagon, all that I will never find again and will no longer hunt for, all is gone, *adiós adiós* so long. And so goodbye to you, *Oyente* patient listener I feel half in love with you. When you sing your songs so close to someone for so long a time and they listen, you feel them listening with love you feel close to that *Oyente* listener. *Oyente* there in the dark I have sung you my own very life please to not forget me. *So long!* Here, take from my lips this kiss whoever you are, dear *Oyente*. So long! *Oyente!* The night falls, I cannot see you! *Oyente!* Have you vanished so quick? *Oyente!* Where are you hiding? I am alone, *la noche baja, la noche cae.* Night falls.

16

A Singer at Large

IT IS NIGHT. THE vision has passed. In the ancient fragile city starlings and bells. The world breaks. Cities fail, towns die. Fields vanish and rivers wither; some wild things can be counted, there are so few. A great mystery may be near. I often dream of water, some of it deep. Sometimes, Uncle Ben, I do not wish to live any longer in this world. Sometimes I want to go home, where we all were. That simple house of early solitude and strangers rises before me, built again, melancholy house of the dark entrance, of the door with the forbidding dark figure. But no one would be there to answer my call at that door: Hello! Hello! And you, Ben, would not be there, even as you were not when I went away through that mysterious portal (it was so grand for a house so plain). Uncle Ben! I have today given you back your darling creature; Arcadio! your creator Ben has come to me through you. And I, both teller and listener, solitary maker, grand and absurd and homesick, who am I? what is life? why are we all here where is God?

Yet you, hearing me—who are you, where have you come from, why have you stayed so long to hear me? *Oyente!* who are we, what is life why are we all here where is God?